the NVQ

assessor
and verifier
HANDBOOK

a practical guide to units A1, A2 and V1

third edition

Jenny Tucker
with Ros Ollin

Publisher's note

Every possible effort has been made to ensure that the information contained in this book is accurate at the time of going to press, and the publishers and authors cannot accept responsibility for any errors or omissions, however caused. No responsibility for loss or damage occasioned to any person acting, or refraining from action, as a result of the material in this publication can be accepted by the editor, the publisher or any of the authors.

First published in Great Britain in 1994 as *The NVQ and GNVQ Assessor Handbook*
Second edition 1997
Third edition 2004 as *The NVQ Assessor and Verifier Handbook*
Reprinted 2005

Kogan Page Limited
120 Pentonville Road
London N1 9JN
United Kingdom
www.kogan-page.co.uk

Kogan Page US
22883 Quicksilver Drive
Sterling VA 20166-2012
USA

© Jenny Tucker and Ros Ollin, 2004

British Library Cataloguing in Publication Data

A CIP record for this book is available from the British Library.

ISBN 0 7494 4047 3

Typeset by JS Typesetting Ltd, Porthcawl, Mid Glamorgan
Printed and bound in Great Britain by Clays Ltd, St Ives plc

Contents

Foreword

Assessors and verifiers are critical to the future credibility, integrity and marketability of N/SVQs. The National Occupational Standards for assessment and verification were approved in December 2001 and heralded a new era in the demands placed upon assessors and verifiers, with a much clearer focus on quality assurance. The Employment National Training Organisation (ENTO) developed the revised standards through extensive consultation with practitioners throughout the United Kingdom, and this theme has been continued in the development of this publication.

This book first appeared some 10 years ago as *The NVQ and GNVQ Assessor Handbook* and proved extremely popular with practitioners. The authors have taken great care to ensure that the format of the original has been maintained but also that the content now reflects the increased demands of the standards and the greater profile that assessment and verification has, compared to then. This version concentrates on the role of the N/SVQ assessor and internal verifier. I am delighted to write the foreword for this publication as I believe passionately in the quality of N/SVQ assessment, and any publication that supports the driving up of standards is critical to the reputation of the standards.

I trust that you will find this publication to be of benefit to you and that it provides you with a source of reference to support your development as an assessor and verifier. Ultimately, the quality of assessment and verification of competence has an impact on the individual being assessed and, where the assessment is leading to accreditation, on the marketability of that qualification. The challenge to us all is to ensure that all candidates achieving an N/SVQ in the future have a qualification that is respected and valued by employers and, more importantly, the candidates themselves.

David Morgan
Director of Marketing and Communications
Employment National Training Organisation

Preface

The introduction of National Vocational Qualifications (NVQs) in the 1990s, with their emphasis on the quality of the outcomes of learning rather than quality delivery, placed assessment practice under the microscope. National Occupational Standards for Training and Development were first produced by the Training and Development Lead Body (TDLB), now superseded by the Employment National Training Organisation (ENTO). After extensive consultation, a new version of the standards, the Learning and Development Standards, was approved in 2002. Like the previous standards, they have been used to create a framework of qualifications comprising both full NVQs and occupational qualifications or small/mini-awards. This framework is reproduced in Appendix 1.

All those assessing and verifying NVQs (and a limited approved range of other competence-based awards) must demonstrate that they have updated their practice to the new standards in order to continue in the role of an assessor or verifier. The new Assessor and Verifier awards are each individual units within the Learning and Development NVQ framework. (See Appendix 6 for the 28 units in the whole suite of Learning and Development NVQs.) Prior to the new standards, the relevant qualifications for assessors and verifiers were commonly known as the 'TDLB D' or 'D3' Units, and are held by most current assessors and verifiers. The new awards are known as the Assessor and Verifier (A&V) awards. ENTO envisaged that these would be used with any competence-based award, though currently usage is primarily for NVQs. Centres wishing to use the A&V awards for assessing other competence-based awards need to get permission from the relevant awarding body, as do assessors who wish to use non-NVQ evidence towards their A&V award.

Holding an Assessor or Verifier award indicates that you are competent to assess and/or verify NVQs in workplaces in England, Wales and Northern Ireland. Scotland has its own set of qualifications (S/NVQs), though the standards are in line with those sanctioned by the QCA, the regulatory body for England and Northern Ireland. The regulatory body for Wales is the ACCAC (Awdurdod Cymwysterau Cwricwlum Ac Asesu Cymru). The Republic of Ireland does not operate the NVQ system.

AIMS OF THIS BOOK

This book aims to provide information and practical advice to anyone wishing to know more about or to obtain these Assessor and Verifier awards. We hope that it will also provide a basis for exploring assessment and verification practice in general and give readers a vehicle for examining their current competence and knowledge.

The book should be of particular use to:

- candidates working towards becoming an accredited assessor or internal verifier for NVQs;
- those wishing to gain a deeper understanding of the principles and processes of NVQ assessment, and of current competence-based assessment practice;
- trainers in NVQ assessment practice who require a reference book for themselves or their candidates;
- those who wish to compare the D3 awards with the A&V awards for the purpose of professional updating.

HOW TO USE THIS BOOK

The book has three parts, each of which is self-contained, as are the chapters. Each chapter has an introductory guide and summary points, for ease of reference.

Part 1 gives a detailed background to assessment and verification processes and sets them firmly in the context of NVQs. It traces the development of the National Occupational Standards (NOS) for Assessment and Verification, and examines the procedures for quality assurance that have been developed over the years by both the predecessors of, and currently, the Department for Education and Skills (DfES), the Qualifications and Curriculum Authority (QCA), the National Training Organisations (NTO) and awarding bodies. It also covers roles of the participants in the assessment and quality assurance process, the requirements on practitioners, the assessment strategy developed by ENTO, and the general underpinning knowledge and understanding for assessment and verification required by both candidates and assessors.

Part 2 is a guide to the standards that assessors and internal verifiers need to follow in their work practice. The standards for external verifiers are included for information, but no detailed guide is given. Part 3 offers practical guidance for candidate-assessors and candidate-internal verifiers working towards the A&V awards. Following the appendices, the book ends with a comprehensive glossary of assessment-related terminology and a listing of support material (further reading, and useful Web sites).

We would urge readers to familiarize themselves with the glossary before turning to the substance of the text, as an understanding of the jargon is vitally important for all concerned. One of the major problems encountered by those coming new to NVQs, or indeed to any occupational area, is in getting to grips with the language and terminology involved. This does not just mean understanding of what the terms mean; it also means feeling an ownership of the language used. The new standards are written in much plainer language than their predecessors, but readers will still wish to mentally translate the terms used into language that appears more familiar and appropriate to their own work context.

Broad and thematic suggestions for further reading are given at the end of the book, rather than references throughout the text, as this is a practical text and we consider it to be of essentially practical use to readers. Throughout the text, we have given a range of examples, including samples of completed documentation and case studies based on real-life situations, to help illustrate points made.

The terms 'assessor-candidate/verifier-candidate' are used throughout to indicate someone taking an assessor (A1 or A2) or internal verifier (V1) award; the term 'candidate' or 'NVQ candidate' refers to those who will be assessed or verified by the assessor-candidate or verifier-candidate. The terms 'assessor' and 'internal verifier' are used to indicate those already qualified to undertake the role.

The new standards clearly define the practice and theory required by assessors and verifiers. We hope that the background discussion, explanation and examples we have given will complement and extend the knowledge and understanding of those engaged in both providing and improving the quality of assessment and verification of National Vocational Qualifications.

Acknowledgements

We wish to thank the many centres, colleagues and candidates with whom we have worked in various capacities over the years. The learning and feedback we have gained from them has been invaluable.

We also wish to thank the Employment National Training Organisation, which has given permission for the use of the standards and other information and especially David Morgan for his help and advice.

Particular thanks to Claire Derrick for the figures, and to Helen Wallis for her timely assistance with formatting, typing and support.

Finally, thanks to our editors at Kogan Page for nagging us to produce this new edition, and their patience in waiting for the final copy!

It should be noted that the views expressed and interpretations of the standards are those of the authors.

Abbreviations

A&V	Assessor and Verifier
ACCAC	Awdurdod Cymwysterau, Cwricwlwm ac Asesu Cymru (Qualifications, Curriculum and Assessment Authority for Wales)
APEL	accreditation of experimental prior learning
APL	accreditation of prior learning
BTEC	Business and Technology Education Council
CDELL	Centre for Developing and Evaluating Lifelong Learning
CIPD	Chartered Institute of Personnel and Development
CPD	continuous professional development
DfES	Department for Education and Skills
ENTO	Employment National Training Organisation
EOSC	Employment Occupational Standards Council
EV	external verifier
HAB	Hospitality Advisory Body
HASAW	Health and Safety at Work (Act)
ICT	information and communications technology
ILB	Industrial Lead Body
IV	internal verifier
IVC	internal verifier co-ordinator
JAB	Joint Awarding Body
NCVQ	National Council for Vocational Qualifications
NTO	National Training Organisation
NVQ	National Vocational Qualification
PSLB	Personnel Standards Lead Body

QCA   Qualifications and Curriculum Authority
TDLB   Training and Development Lead Body
TUDSB   Trade Union Sector Development Body

Part 1

Knowledge Requirements

Introduction: The Background to NVQs and to the Assessor and Verifier Awards

The intention behind National Vocational Qualifications (NVQs) is to have a coherent national system of qualifications, related to specific occupational areas, that can be easily understood, gives credit for what people can do as well as what they know, and can be achieved independently from any formal programme of learning. The assessments are done in the workplace, as candidates learn and perform 'on the job', though they may attend classes for theory and practice, eg at a college of further education, or in an employer's own training centre. This represents a major shift from the traditional model of apprenticeships, in which assessment was theoretical and apprentices often watched rather than performed tasks. NVQs have been designed to assess the ability to perform a particular job or tasks, without having to take into account the way in which that ability was learnt. This makes them particularly suitable for those practising and experienced employees who are skilled in their occupation but who have no formal qualifications.

The development of occupational standards and their related vocational qualifications are an important part of the government's skills strategy, designed to equip Britain with a well-qualified workforce able to meet the economic challenges of the 21st century.

BACKGROUND TO NVQS

In the early 1980s, both government and industry recognized the need to improve the skills of the workforce to enable Britain to compete more effectively in overseas markets. To make this improvement possible, a number of factors needed to be addressed. There had to be a systematic identification of what skills were actually needed, an increase in training or retraining where necessary, and a straightforward and coherent qualifications framework to provide formal recognition of the skills acquired.

In 1986 the government established the National Council for Vocational Qualifications (NCVQ) to oversee the development of a new qualifications framework based on nationally agreed standards of performance and covering different occupational areas. In order to determine these national standards, Industrial Lead Bodies (ILB) covering different occupational areas were set up. These comprised representatives from employers, industry, related professional bodies and trade unions.

Each ILB was given the responsibility for leading the development of a detailed profile of skills and knowledge required at all levels in the related occupational area. These detailed specifications were based on what an individual had to demonstrate to be considered competent when carrying out work in a particular job role. They also laid down a minimum national standard of performance that had to be met. The ILB then formed these standards into vocational qualifications at different levels, which were approved by the NCVQ. Different awarding bodies such as City & Guilds, the Business and Technology Education Council (BTEC), the Electricity Training Association and the Management Verification Consortium then offered these qualifications.

During the 1990s various reforms took place. These resulted in the merging of some of the awarding bodies and a consequent contraction in their number, the replacement of the Lead Bodies by the National Training Organisations (NTOs), and the replacement of the NCVQ by the Qualifications and Curriculum Authority (QCA). National Occupational Standards are currently devised by industry-led NTOs.

The awarding bodies construct qualifications from the standards, and gain approval for these qualifications via the QCA. Once the qualification is approved, it appears on the QCA's database of national qualifications, and can be offered to candidates via centres that meet the criteria of the relevant awarding bodies. When NVQs are offered, it is a condition of centre approval that the quality assurance system for the centre has approved assessment and internal verification practice. Assessors and verifiers must operate to the criteria laid down in the Assessor and Verifier (A&V) standards, and meet any additional criteria set by the NTOs in their own assessment strategy.

Since late 2001, NTOs have gradually been merging into broader Sector Skills Councils, which bring together different branches of related industries.

KEY FEATURES OF NVQS

Prior to the introduction of NVQs, occupational and vocationally related qualifications were linked to training courses, apprenticeships or programmes of study, with students studying for their qualification or certificate either full- or part-time. Although many courses were well taught, one major criticism was that they concentrated too much on what academic programme designers wanted to include, or what had traditionally been expected of an employee, and not enough on what was actually needed at work in the new global economy.

NVQs are intended to be firmly based in the work context and designed for accrediting the skills of working people and providing a system for identifying where skills and knowledge need to be acquired, or updated. They take as their starting point the question 'What skills and knowledge do particular occupational areas need?' They are then concerned with measuring, assessing and accrediting whether someone can actually perform competently within that occupational area. NVQs:

- are based on an analysis of work roles in terms of what functions need to be performed;
- are led by employers and industry-specific professional bodies – not by 'education';
- focus on *the ability to do the job competently* and *not* on whether someone is as good as or better than someone else;
- define five different levels of competence (see Figure I.1, page 7);
- concentrate on assessment of outcomes.

The NVQ framework

The NVQ framework consists of 11 occupational areas. Each occupational area has its range of occupational NVQs at a variety of levels. The A&V units are from the range of qualifications and mini-awards from the occupational area designated as 'Developing and extending knowledge and skill'.

Each NVQ has a three- to five-year 'product life', after which it is subject to revision. New and revised NVQs are therefore constantly coming on stream. Mini-qualifications are small groups of standards. The A&V units fall into this category, as each consists of just one unit. Certificate Awards are developed from small groups of units (see Appendix 5). A full NVQ often has 10 or more units. All NVQ qualifications developed from standards need to be approved by the QCA to ensure that they fit into the overall qualifications framework at the appropriate levels.

This framework is a national system for ordering qualifications according to their complexity of academic content or job role. There are five levels in all, plus an entry level. NVQs in Learning and Development are all at level 3 or above. The Assessor awards are at level 3 and the Verifier awards are at level 4. This means that candidates for the Internal Verifier award need to be in a position of managing internal verification procedures, and managing assessors as part of that quality assurance process.

- *Level 1* – competence that involves the application of knowledge in the performance of a range of varied work activities, most of which may be routine or predictable.
- *Level 2* – competence that involves the application of knowledge in a significant range of varied work activities, performed in a variety of contexts. Some of the activities are complex or non-routine, and there is some individual responsibility or autonomy. Collaboration with others, perhaps through membership of a work group or team, may often be a requirement.
- *Level 3* – competence that involves the application of knowledge in a broad range of varied work activities performed in a wide variety of contexts, most of which are complex and non-routine. There is considerable responsibility and autonomy, and control by and guidance from others is often required.
- *Level 4* – competence that involves the application of knowledge in a broad range of complex technical or professional work activities performed in a wide variety of contexts and with a substantial degree of personal responsibility and autonomy. Responsibility for the work of others and the allocation of resources is often present.
- *Level 5* – competence that involves the application of a significant range of fundamental principles across a wide and often unpredictable variety of contexts. Very substantial personal autonomy and often significant responsibility for the work of others and for the allocation of substantial resources feature strongly, as do personal accountabilities for analysis and diagnosis, design, planning, execution and evaluation.

The 11 occupational framework areas covered by NVQs are:

- tending animals, plants and land;
- extracting and providing natural resources;
- constructing;
- engineering;
- manufacturing;
- transporting;
- providing goods and services;

Qualifications for work
(choices for 16-year-olds)

Postgraduate degrees/diplomas	Postgraduate degrees/diplomas	NVQ levels 4/5
Degrees in academic disciplines	Vocationally orientated degrees/diplomas	NVQ levels 4/5
A/AS	GNVQ level 3	NVQ levels 3/4
GCSE	GNVQ levels 1/2	NVQ level 1/2

Figure I.1 A mapping of current qualifications

- providing health, social and protective services;
- providing business services;
- communicating;
- developing and extending knowledge and skill.

There is no programme of learning or syllabus built into an NVQ qualification. This does not mean that learning programmes are not devised for NVQs. NVQ candidates often attend a further education college or training centre to gain the background knowledge and to practise their skills, and may find themselves on an NVQ course. This may be on a day-release basis, or be full-time with real work experience built into the programme.

Up-to-date information on the full range of NVQs offered can be found on the NVQ database, available on the QCA's Web site.

KEY SKILLS

Six Key Skills qualifications give employees and any student the opportunity to demonstrate the underpinning key skills that are needed for effective performance at each of the five qualifications levels. Application of Number, Communication and Information Technology are perhaps the most crucial, as an employee's level of achievement in these Key Skills is often fundamental to his or her ability to work accurately and efficiently. Team Building, Problem

Solving and Improvement of Own Learning and Performance are complementary to the core Key Skills, and offer candidates the opportunity to show their additional people-based skills that make them effective and valuable employees. Most qualifications are now mapped against the Key Skills specifications, so candidates can demonstrate many of the Key Skills competences through obtaining their occupational or vocationally related qualification. Candidates who start an NVQ or any other qualification are likely to be given a Key Skills assessment as part of their induction. Modern Apprenticeships require candidates to achieve in Key Skills.

MODERN APPRENTICESHIPS, TECHNICAL CERTIFICATES AND CRAFT CERTIFICATES

In 2003 there were 14 occupational areas covered by Craft Certificates. These are:

- art and design;
- business;
- health and social care;
- leisure and tourism;
- manufacturing;
- construction and the built environment;
- hospitality and catering;
- science;
- engineering;
- information technology;
- media: communications and production;
- retail and distribution;
- land and environment;
- the performing arts and entertainment industries.

Craft and Technical certificates are vocationally related qualifications that are taught off the job, and are subject to some external assessment. They are for those who are not able to practise a particular skill in the workplace, or who prefer a more traditional approach to learning.

Since 2000, Technical Certificates have been linked specifically to Modern Apprenticeships, and are a mandatory part of the Advanced Modern Apprenticeship. They provide the theoretical underpinning for the knowledge and assessment in the Modern Apprenticeship NVQs.

The certificates often have a broader educational focus within the chosen occupational area. Students learn through programmes that emphasize the development of key skills as well as occupational skills. However, in spite of

NVQs	Technical or Craft Certificates
Occupational competence	Broad-based vocational education
Assessment of competence and knowledge in workplace	Assessment of theoretical knowledge
Standards devised by industry	Syllabus devised by awarding bodies in consultation with industry
No grading – only competent or not yet competent	Grading at end: pass/merit/distinction

Figure I.2 Similarities and differences between NVQs and Technical or Craft Certificates

the differences in the way NVQs and technical or craft certificates are delivered and assessed, there are still some significant similarities in assessment practice.

Both NVQs and technical or craft certificates are based on the same principles of assessment. They are both assessed to national standards, on the basis of evidence demonstrated and presented by the candidate, and both are committed to promoting equality of access to assessment regardless of disability, geographical location, religion, ethnic group or gender. Hence the assessment process and the considerations to be taken into account are very similar in spite of the 'cultural' differences between work and education.

The QCA and the awarding bodies wish to ensure consistency in assessment methods and practices because of the similarities in the assessment process, together with the intention to maximize transferability within the qualification framework. This is why all assessors and verifiers for both NVQs and technical certificates are expected to achieve an appropriate Assessor or Verifier award, which can demonstrate their ability to carry out their particular role in quality assurance.

OBJECTIONS TO NVQS

NVQs are not primarily concerned with *how* someone learnt to do something, or what *training* they received, but whether that person is competent in the workplace. Some of those who obtained their own qualifications 'pre-NVQ' still find it difficult to understand that the assessment of competence in the workplace is as valid a method of assessment as the craft apprenticeship examination. The NVQ focus on whether someone can perform a job of work to a required standard with the associated understanding and knowledge that successful performance in the workplace requires can seem to them to be of less worth than 'craft apprenticeships' or attendance on traditional vocational training courses. In fact, many candidates taking NVQ qualifications do follow programmes of study related to the underpinning knowledge and skills for their qualification, in addition to their workplace assessment. It is only at level 3 that candidates will be able to demonstrate that they have similar levels of knowledge and skill to those who have been through the full traditional apprenticeship and craft certificate programmes. Currently (February 2004), only 3 per cent of the workforce have achieved NVQs at level 3, and just 12 per cent of the workforce have achieved at level 2. There is obviously some considerable way to go before the government targets for a qualified workforce are met.

The NVQ assessment-driven model has produced the same kind of arguments as those related to the National Curriculum, ie that too much time is being spent on testing at the expense of learning. We feel that this concern is based on a misunderstanding of the nature of NVQs. It is important to emphasize again that NVQs are a means of *accrediting* learning or experience, unlike qualifications such as A levels or GCSEs, which are closely linked to formal programmes of learning. So, whereas these concerns are relevant to educational programmes in which the 'learning' time allocated to a course of study is being taken up with tests, we do not believe that they are relevant to NVQs, in which learning and assessment can be, and perhaps should be, divorced. As an illustration of this, suppose that an individual has done the same type of work for five years. During that time she will have learnt a great deal. Maybe she will have been on a course to improve her skills and knowledge, yet she is likely to have no formal qualifications to recognize what she can do, ie the *practical end product* of learning or experience. The important factor for an employer will in reality be not how or when the learning took place, but how competently that individual can now perform and whether her performance is based on sound underpinning knowledge and understanding. NVQs provide accreditation of that competence through the opportunity to match current occupational competence against the standards, improve where necessary, and get accreditation for that competence and knowledge while remaining at work.

Others have raised doubts about the process of functional analysis by which the standards have been developed. A particular concern is that this process provides too narrow and mechanical a framework with which to analyse jobs that are complex in nature, or to deal with work that involves professional ethics and values. A related issue is that NVQs are not concerned with how much knowledge someone has about an occupational area, only how far that knowledge informs their ability to perform a particular job of work competently. This raises questions about the nature of knowledge and whether occupational areas have a 'body' of knowledge that should provide an overall context for the skills required, and that loses its coherence if separated into discrete areas and linked closely with specific competences. Indeed, the issue of 'competence' in general has produced an energetic and passionate debate, with opponents of NVQs criticizing them for supporting a mechanistic approach that leaves no room for identification of excellence, and that encourages mediocrity rather than high performance. It is unfortunate that in some instances, NVQs have been delivered and assessed by centres in a mechanistic way, with candidates never getting a holistic view of the qualification. The recent work done by the QCA, ENTO and the awarding bodies should have a significant effect on eliminating this poor practice. Various reports (Smithers, 1993; Beaumont, 1996; Dearing, 1996; see Figure I.3) highlighted a range of real and perceived problems with the assessment of qualifications, and raised many issues for employers, providers and government agencies. The QCA commissioned the Nottingham Centre for Developing and Evaluating Lifelong Learning (CDELL) to investigate a range of issues around NVQs. These have focused on the reliability of NVQs, their validity and transferability, and fair assessment, and make interesting reading. Action resulting from the findings of the reports caused radical changes in quality assurance practice for NVQs. The introduction of the new standards on internal verification, the new NVQ Code of Practice with clear sanctions for non-compliant centres, and the coming together of the larger awarding bodies to put out joint guidance on internal verification (the JAB Guidelines) have now made for a sound system of occupational training and assessment.

1981 New Training Initiative (Manpower Service Commission [MSC])
Identified need to increase skills of workforce to cope with new patterns of working, developments in new technology and increased competition from overseas. First mention of need for 'Standards of a new kind'.

1986 *Review of Vocational Qualifications: A Report by the Working Group* (MSC and Department of Education and Science)
Concluded that there was a low take-up of vocational qualifications. Perceived by employers as relying too much on theory as opposed to practice. Confusion and overlap on the provision available, with difficulties in access, progression and transfer of credits. Problems with methods of assessment and little recognition of learning outside formal programmes.

1986 *Working Together: Education and Training* (Government White Paper)
Proposed the development of new qualifications based on national standards defined by industry and operating within a coherent qualifications structure.

1986 National Council for Vocational Qualifications (NCVQ) established
To carry out proposals from the White Paper including the accreditation of standards, development of new qualifications framework, development of NVQs, liaison with awarding bodies and monitoring of quality assurance procedures. The NCVQ was set up as an independent body with initial government funding covering England, Wales and Northern Ireland. It has no legal powers but must promote the new vocational initiative through co-operation with relevant bodies. The Scottish Council for Vocational Education Training (SCOTVEC) has the same remit in Scotland.

1986 New Occupational Standards Branch created at MSC
Given responsibility for setting up industry lead bodies to develop occupational standards. Where possible, the lead bodies built on existing organizations, eg Industrial Training Boards such as the Construction Industry Training Board (CITB).

1988 *Employment for the 1990s* (Government White Paper)
Reaffirmed the need for standards and qualifications based on competence and recognized by employers. Proposed establishment of local Training and Enterprise Councils (TECs) to be responsible at local level for the planning and delivery of vocational training and enterprise programmes.

1990 Training Agency (formerly MSC) becomes absorbed
Absorbed in the Training, Enterprise and Education Directorate (TEED) at the Department of Employment

1991 *Education and Training for the 21st Century* (Government White Paper)
Proposed that General National Vocational Qualifications designed to provide broad-based vocational preparation should be introduced into the national qualification framework.

1992 National Targets for Education and Training announced
Targets for young people, adults and employers.

1994 *Competitiveness: Helping Businesses to Win* (Government White Paper)
£300 million to be spent on strengthening education and training. Review

of NVQs announced to ensure they 'stayed up to date and continued to observe strict standards'. Five hundred NVQs covering 150 occupations represented 80% of all jobs now approved.

1995 **Department for Education and Employment (DfEE) created (July) from merger of the Department for Education and the Employment Department**

1996 **(Jan) *Review of 100 NVQs/SVQs* Report (Chair: Gordon Beaumont)**
Supported NVQ/SVQ concept. Indicated widespread concern over rigour and consistency of assessment and complexity of language of standards. Eighty per cent of employers considered that competence-based standards were right for vocational qualifications.

1996 **(March) *Review of Qualifications for 16- to 19-Year-Olds* Report (Chair: Sir Ron Dearing)**
Made a large number of recommendations for improving current provision. Endorsed the Beaumont review. Changed the term 'Core Skills' to 'Key Skills' and suggested that Key Skills Requirements should be considered when designing NVQs. Recommended the merger of the NCVQ and the Schools Curriculum and Assessment Authority (SCAA) to support a cohesive academic/vocational qualifications framework.

1996 **Education Act: Department for Education and Skills (DfES) created**

1996 ***Competitiveness: Creating the Enterprise Centre of Europe* (Government White Paper)**
Emphasizes need for providers of training and qualifications to undergo rigorous quality assurance procedures.

1997 **Qualifications and Curriculum Authority set up**

1997 **Employment National Training Organisation (EmpNTO)**
Formed from merger of Employment Occupational Standards Council and Occupational Health and Safety Lead Body, and is the first NTO to represent different groups found throughout all sectors of industry. *Publication of External Verification of NVQs by QCA.*

1998 **(March) QCA publishes *Internal Verification of NVQs, Assessing NVQs* and *Revised Common Accord***
Responsibility for National Occupational Standards devolved to regulatory bodies.

1999 **QCA publishes *Developing Assessment Strategies for NVQs***

2000 **Learning and Skills Act**

2000 **QCA publishes *The NVQ Code of Practice***
Clearly sets out ways in which organizations should be accredited to run and assess NVQs. It includes a Tariff of Sanctions to be applied by external verifiers where centres are not in compliance with the code.

2002 **Sector Skills Development Agency (SSDA)**
Set up by government to fund and support new Sector Skills Councils. Joint remit for vocational qualification system given to QCA, LSC, SSDA.

2002 **Joint Awarding Body Guidance on Internal Verification of NVQs**
Document backed by awarding bodies, which states how internal verification will be approached by them all.

2002 EmpNTO publishes the Learning and Development Standards to replace the TDLB Standards
Review of National Qualifications Framework.
2003 EmpNTO rebadges as ENTO
Publication by DfES of *21st Century Skills: Realising our potential – individuals, employers, nation.* Sets out a national skills strategy.
2004 (Jan) QCA report evaluating A & V awards covering six awarding bodies
2004 (Feb) First meeting of the Lifelong Learning Executive Group Sector Skills Council

Figure I.3   Background to NVQs

1

The Organizations Involved in the Development and Delivery of National Standards

This chapter explains the role and functions of the key bodies involved with the Assessor and Verifier awards (the A&V awards), gives information on the national occupational standards and qualifications system, and discusses the importance of quality assurance and the implications of the NVQ Code of Practice. It then provides guidance on the services offered by accredited centres. The chapter contains a number of abbreviations and jargon words. The glossary explains these terms.

THE REGULATORY AUTHORITIES AND THE LEARNING AND SKILLS COUNCIL

The regulatory authorities are the bodies for England and Wales, Northern Ireland and Scotland that determine the regulations for standards, quality and awards for the UK. The body affecting England is the Qualifications and Curriculum Authority (QCA), formed from a merger of regional bodies in 2000. Wales and Scotland have their own regulatory bodies. QCA has sole regulatory responsibility for NVQs offered in Northern Ireland. The Learning and Skills Council (LSC) funds post-16 and work-based learning in England and Wales. Approved qualifications on the QCA's database receive different levels of funding according to whether they require additional resources for equipment or type of learner. Funding is currently allocated according to enrolments, those retained over the course, and those completing programmes. It is in the interests of both the organization, from a financial point of view, and the learner, from an achievement point of view, to ensure that the learner is matched to a programme whereby he or she is able to achieve and gain a recognized qualification.

The QCA NVQ Code of Practice and quality assurance

Inevitably, as the number of accredited centres offering awards, designated and qualified assessors, and candidates for awards increased, so did differences of opinion and of practice between centres, which was unhelpful both to candidates and to perceived and actual quality.

In August 1993 the NCVQ introduced the Common Accord, which was 'intended to enhance the quality and cost effectiveness of NVQ assessment and verification processes operated by Awarding Bodies' (NCVQ, 1993). The QCA brought out a revised version, 'The Awarding Bodies' Common Accord', in July 1997. In September 2000 the regulatory authorities published the 'Arrangements for the statutory regulation of external qualifications in England, Wales and Northern Ireland'.

The NVQ Code of Practice, produced by the QCA and published in 2002, supplements the above document, and replaces the Common Accord. The NVQ Code of Practice sets out:

- agreed principles and practice for the assessment and quality assurance of NVQs and NVQ units;
- the responsibilities of NVQ Awarding Bodies and their accredited centres in respect of the administration, assessment and verification of NVQs and NVQ units;
- the basis upon which the Qualifications, Curriculum and Assessment Authority for Wales (ACCAC) and the QCA will systematically monitor the performance of awarding bodies in maintaining the quality and standards across the NVQs they offer;
- the sanctions to be applied to centres that do not comply with the code of practice.

See Appendix 2 for an explanation of the sanctions.

All accredited centres should have a copy of the NVQ Code of Practice, which can also be obtained from the QCA, and all assessors and internal verifiers should have their own copies. The Code of Practice lays down the *minimum* requirements for each assessment and verification role, and centres must have staff qualified to these minimum standards.

The Joint Awarding Body Guidance on Internal Verification

The Joint 'Awarding Body Guidance on Internal Verification of NVQs', published in 2001, was the work of a steering group of a DfEE national project, and supplements the previous QCA guide 'Internal verification of NVQs', published in 1997. The guidance aims to increase the reliability of assessment practice across the country, and raised the profile and role of the internal quality assurance processes and staff in terms of ensuring that national standards are met, and in minimizing risk. Again, all centres and internal verifiers should have a copy of, and use, this document for guidance.

Assessment strategies

The regulatory authorities decided that each NVQ should have an assessment strategy, which must apply in all cases. Each NVQ now has an assessment strategy, devised by the NTO which devised the standards from which the NVQ or mini-award has been constructed. Along with the revised standards, ENTO has a Learning and Development Assessment Strategy (reproduced in Appendix 3) that needs to be followed and implemented by approved centres.

THE ROLE OF NTOS AND AWARDING BODIES IN THE DEVELOPMENT OF NATIONAL STANDARDS AND NVQS

National Training Organisations and ENTO

The tasks of identifying, defining and revising the standards comprising NVQs are now undertaken by NTOs, which have taken over from the disbanded Lead Bodies. Membership of NTOs comprises representation from the public sector, from industry, professional bodies, employer and trades associations, and practitioners.

National Standards for Training and Development were first issued in 1992 and comprehensively revised in 1994, under the direction of the then Training and Development Lead Body (TDLB). In November 1994, three lead bodies that were concerned with generic skills across a range of broadly related occupations – the TDLB, the Personnel Standards Lead Body (PSLB) and the Trade Union Sector Development Body (TUDSB) – were amalgamated to form the Employment Occupational Standards Council (EOSC). The EOSC took forward the work started by the original three lead bodies to provide a comprehensive range of qualifications. The Employment National Training Organisation (ENTO, formerly EmpNTO) has now replaced the EOSC.

ENTO's mission is about 'developing the competence of people who work with people'. The NTO is responsible for standards for Learning and Development, Health and Safety, Personnel, Managing Work-related Violence, and Trade Unions, as well as for Advice and Guidance organizations, the publishing of Professional Development Guides, and having responsibility for the matrix quality standard (an organizational standard like Investors in People). ENTO is also responsible for The Learning Network, a Web-based network for assessors and verifiers, where up-to-the-minute information on assessment and verification is available, as are details of updating and training courses, along with an online chat facility for those who are registered members.

Awarding bodies

Awarding bodies devise a wide range of qualifications, syllabuses, tests, exams and pass criteria, and employ external examiners, moderators and/or verifiers. Awarding bodies are accredited by the QCA to offer NVQs. Assessors and verifiers who assess units from the occupational area of Learning and Development (which include the A&V awards) need to be qualified in this area through a relevant education or training award. NVQ assessors and verifiers must be competent not only in the skills and knowledge related to advising, assessing or verifying, but also in their occupational field such as engineering, providing business services, or agriculture and amenity horticulture.

With respect to NVQs, once National Occupational Standards and assessment strategies have been developed and agreed by the NTOs and QCA, awarding bodies interpret them into qualifications and programmes. They have the responsibility for developing the evidence requirements for each qualification, of registering candidates for qualifications and awarding certificates for qualifications. This last function means that quality assurance is a major part of their work. Awarding bodies approve centres to offer NVQs (and other qualifications), and are responsible for ensuring that assessment, verification and monitoring are carried out in accordance with the Code of Practice and the advice issued by the NTOs and QCA. They recruit, train and appoint external verifiers to do much of this work. External verifiers have to operate at the V2 award standard (see Chapter 8), which is offered only by the awarding bodies themselves. Many awarding bodies also sponsor the development of training and assessment materials, produce publications, arrange training for programme deliverers and assessors, and provide consultancy.

There are currently 8 awarding bodies offering the full Learning and Development NVQs and 20 who offer some of the A&V units as occupational qualifications. 4 awarding bodies offer 9 certificate qualifications particularly aimed at workbased providers, such as 'Coaching Learners in the Workplace'. The ENTO web site gives full information on availability of qualifications.

The Dearing review of 1996 suggested a rationalization of awarding bodies, since the monitoring of the large number in existence had become an almost impossible task. The number is still large, at over 100, but there has been some rationalization over the years, notably as regards the large public examination bodies. For example, OCR was formed from the merger of the Oxford and

---

QUALITY ASSURANCE FOR NVQS

Qualifications and Curriculum Authority (QCA)
National Training Organisations
Awarding bodies
External verifiers
Internal verifiers
Assessors

Figure 1.1 NVQ quality assurance

Cambridge, London and the Royal Society of Arts awarding bodies. The QCA's Web site gives details of awarding bodies and the NVQs they offer.

The final link in the quality assurance chain is the QCA itself. All awarding bodies have to apply for accreditation and then submit themselves for re-accreditation on a regular basis. If the QCA is not satisfied with an awarding body's management of the quality assurance procedures for assessment and verification, its accreditation to award NVQs will be withdrawn.

CHOOSING AN AWARDING BODY

Candidates and organizations sometimes wonder which is the 'best' awarding body with which to register, and this indicates that in the public mind there is still some sort of perceived hierarchy or status that attaches to qualifications awarded by particular bodies. Many candidates will take their NVQs and A&V awards through the awarding body related to their profession, eg the Institute of the Motor Industry (IMI) or the Association of Accounting Technicians (AAT). Most candidates joining a general training programme in, for example, a college of further education will be registered with the awarding body that has accredited the centre where they are studying. This will often be one of the large generic awarding bodies such as City & Guilds, OCR or Edexcel (formed from the merger of BTEC and London Examinations).

There have been a number of comparative studies done between the services and materials provided by awarding bodies, and these indicate that each awarding body has different strengths and appeal. Professional trainers, for example, may prefer to take their awards through the Chartered Institute of Personnel and Development (CIPD), which is also one of the professional organizations for trainers, and whose process for the awards particularly encourages reflective learning and continuous professional development. Catering assessors might be more inclined to use City & Guilds, which is well known for its Hospitality and Catering awards, or the Hospitality Advisory Body (HAB).

As already mentioned, a complete list of awarding bodies offering assessor and verifier qualifications can be found on the QCA's Web site.

ACCREDITED CENTRES

Accredited centres are organizations approved by awarding bodies to provide advice, guidance and training for particular awards, and to register, assess, internally verify and accredit candidates. They are subject to external verification from the awarding body, and to auditing from the QCA. It may well be that potential candidates already work for an organization accredited to offer the required qualifications, in which case they may or may not have a choice of accredited centre.

Some organizations wanting their staff to take A&V awards will prefer to choose centres that offer a range of qualifications relevant to the work of their staff. For example, employers with staff following self-development programmes may want an A&V centre that also offers CIPD awards, whereas others will want to choose a centre that specializes in A&V awards and can deliver these for all their staff, irrespective of their occupational area. Yet others will choose a centre they feel happy with, irrespective of any other factors.

There are clear criteria laid down in the Code of Practice for the approval of centres. All centres should be operating to the NVQ Code of Practice. A centre may have several sites all operating under the same systems. Awarding bodies will be pleased to supply lists of accredited centres.

Services provided by approved centres

Centres deal with candidate registrations, allocation of candidates to assessors, assessment and certification paperwork, and usually any associated support needed by candidates. Many offer the facility for accrediting prior learning. The variety and quality of the training, support and assessment offered by the centre with which they register is probably the biggest factor in candidates' ability to profit fully from the process associated with gaining an award.

Candidates or employers need to satisfy themselves concerning the amount of support offered, the ways in which competence and knowledge will be assessed and verified in the workplace, and who will be doing this, and the time that candidates are expected to take to achieve their NVQ or mini-award. The centre should have a range of supporting resources such as reading materials relating to assessment and to the occupational standards with which candidates will be involved. Most centres produce a variety of back-up materials to supplement those provided by the awarding bodies and NTOs. (The list of further reading at the end of the book gives an idea of publications available that can provide added support.)

The client or organization concerned will also need to check, before registering, that the centre can provide the full range of services they need. Centres vary very considerably in their physical and human resources, as well as in their ability to help candidates to achieve within acceptable timescales. The following list gives an idea of the range of services that are likely to be offered by accredited centres:

- briefing sessions – introducing the awards and the NVQ system;
- planning workshops – guiding candidates in ways to demonstrate competence;
- knowledge and understanding workshops – training in background information;
- open learning – background materials that can be studied at the candidate's convenience;
- individual support – one-to-one advice, review and feedback sessions;
- group support – either tutored sessions or self-support groups;
- workplace assessment – assessors visiting the candidates' work environment to assess competence;
- resource-based learning centres – computers with Internet access and reading materials;
- accreditation of prior learning (APL) – staff trained to check this and provide action plans.

Costs

Timescale and cost are difficult to estimate, because they depend on the individual awarding body's charges, the rates charged by different centres, the amount of support required by individuals, and the ability of the staff providing the support, training and assessment. Some candidates have taken just months to complete a whole NVQ, whereas others have taken years to complete a couple of units. We estimate that assessor-candidates who are new to NVQ assessment could need to spend around 15 hours developing their underpinning knowledge of competence-based assessment through reading appropriate publications and visiting Web sites, and talking to relevant people such as their workplace supervisor, their internal verifier or a mentor. Planning the assessment for an NVQ unit will probably take around an hour per unit initially, and less time as the process develops, the candidate becomes more familiar with the standards, and it becomes clear how evidence covering a range of units can be assessed holistically. The majority of the time, and therefore costs, should ideally be on workplace observations, feedback following these, and professional discussion. Skilled planning is needed to ensure that the observation sessions are efficient and effective. Motivation, being well briefed, an overall grasp of the assessment system in use, and plentiful opportunities for demonstrating competence via observation are the keys to efficient and effective accreditation. (See Chapter 9 for more details of assessment in different work contexts.)

Costs incurred will be of both variable and fixed types, depending on whether they relate to 'products' such as registration and certification, or processes such as assessment time. These will vary according to the procedures of the awarding body and the assessment centre selected. Some of the expenses incurred by centres, such as centre approval fees, are likely to be passed on to candidates in some way. Costs are sometimes kept down by centres running group sessions rather than one-to-one sessions; candidates will have to consider whether the financial saving is worth the loss of individual tuition and support. If candidates find that they are spending 'non-work' time on 'portfolio building', it is likely that their centre is not using its assessors as well as it might to lead the assessment of competence. Candidates would be advised to renegotiate their assessment plans so that the assessor uses more work-based evidence and professional discussion to make his or her assessment judgements.

Charges related to assessment will include all or some of the following:

- centre approval and registration;
- candidate registration (per unit or award);
- support materials, standards packs;
- support workshops;
- workplace assessment;
- unit summative assessment;
- internal and external verification;
- administration and travel costs.

Currently, only around 50 per cent of candidates complete the NVQs for which they register. If achievement is your priority, it may be that a centre that charges more, but is firmly rooted in effective assessor-led workplace assessment, may ultimately be the most efficient choice. 'Shopping around' to find the most appropriate package is recommended both for individuals and for organizations.

SUMMARY

This chapter should have helped you with the following:

- understanding the role of NTOs and awarding bodies in the development of national standards and NVQs;
- understanding the NVQ framework and the structure of qualifications in England and Wales;
- awareness of the national quality assurance systems for NVQs, including the NVQ Code of Practice and the Joint Awarding Body Guidance;
- the role of awarding bodies;
- understanding the purposes and functions of accredited centres.

2

Assessment: Procedures, Knowledge and Skills Needed to Perform the Roles

All those involved in the assessment and verification of NVQs need a high level of skill in order to do their jobs competently and effectively. These skills are not purely mechanical: they involve the ability to analyse, to choose appropriately, to transfer across different contexts, to be sensitive to individual needs and to absorb and communicate substantial amounts of information. The ability to carry out such activities can only occur in conjunction with the knowledge and understanding of different methods and practices involved in assessment, of different strategies for working with people and of some awareness of the ethical context in which anyone in a potentially powerful role should operate. Some professionals, such as training managers or lecturers, carry out a whole range of tasks, while others specialize, eg in assessing or mentoring. This chapter explains different types and methods of assessment, including consideration of some of the more 'people-based' skills that are needed for assessment and verification.

TYPES OF ASSESSMENT

Criterion-referenced assessment

NVQs are criterion-referenced systems of assessment – that is, the candidate is assessed against a set of pre-established criteria. These criteria represent a consensus of opinion over what forms the basis of an 'acceptable' standard. In a sense, all occupational areas are already based on criterion-referenced systems. For example, if a car were having its brakes mended, the owner would want to feel confident that the mechanic was working to an acceptable set of standards within the motor industry. Similarly, a patient being looked after by a nurse would want to feel that the nurse was performing duties to a standard required by any hospital in the country. The creation of sets of national standards for different occupational areas is a reflection of what has tradition-ally occurred in practice, although there is always professional controversy, of course, over whether the criteria identified in the standards are the right ones.

In assessments made against criteria, there are only two possible outcomes for a candidate. They can be judged either competent against the criteria or not yet competent against the criteria. For example, in vehicle body repair, a candidate fitting replacement body panels either *does* or *does not* position the replacement components according to the vehicle manufacturer's specifica-tions. In the first case he or she *is* competent against that criterion, and in the second case he or she is *not yet* competent against that criterion. However, there are obviously many situations where the judgement of competence is more problematic, particularly where the language appears to allow for subjective judgement, and we will be covering these later in this chapter. In criterion-referenced assessment there is no limit to the numbers of candidates who can be judged competent, as long as they meet the full requirements of the standards.

Norm-referenced assessment

Traditional academic programmes are based on norm-referenced systems in which the achievement of the candidate is judged in comparison to the achievement of other candidates. Hence in programmes such as A levels and GCSEs, candidates who obtain an 'A' grade are judged to be better than candidates who have obtained a 'C' grade. Norm-referenced systems have their basis in the idea that a few will do well, most will do averagely and some will do poorly. That means there is an expectation that a few people will get 'A' grades, a large number of people will get 'C' grades and some will get 'E' or even 'F' grades (see Figure 2.1). If one year it turned out that a large number of people obtained 'A' grades, the system would be studied closely and revised.

Either the examinations would be made more difficult, or the examiners making the assessments would be told to assess more strictly. Hence there is no real notion of 'fixed' standards. Every year, when the A level and GCSE results are published, and the numbers passing the examination increases, there is a debate about whether standards are falling. It could be that improved teaching methods and revision support enable more candidates to do better. However, only a certain number are *expected* to get top grades. More candidates achieving well can skew some dependent processes – for example, making it more difficult to get into particular universities because there are more students with good grades available than there are places.

To clarify a major problem in the norm-referenced system, let us consider our previous example of the patient being looked after by the nurse. It would be no consolation to the patient that the nurse was the best in the country if the general standards of nursing care nationally were inadequate and the nurse was merely the best out of a very poorly skilled profession. The problem with norm referencing, then, is that comparisons only suggest that someone is better or worse in a particular group, and do not suggest what the minimum standard for performance or achievement actually is.

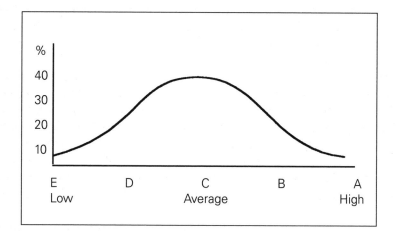

Figure 2.1 Performance distribution curve

However, it is true that many employers and higher education establishments do place an emphasis on the achievement of high grades, and that norm referencing does provide a means of distinguishing between individual employees or students.

Formative assessment

Every time candidates receive a judgement on their performance that will cause them to alter certain aspects of it, they are receiving formative assessment, ie assessment that 'forms' their development towards a certain desired goal, just as a metalworker 'forms' a hot piece of metal towards a certain desired shape. This type of assessment takes place on a continuous basis – sometimes formally, but very often informally. Formative assessment that is carried out helpfully and sympathetically can play a large part in motivating candidates, particularly those unsure of their own abilities. The recording of formative assessment outcomes by the assessor will lead to a gradual build-up of positively assessed competences and associated knowledge, which will give candidates a clear understanding as to what aspects of performance they still need to work on.

Case studies in formative assessment

1. A candidate working in a restaurant is constantly receiving feedback on his performance by the head waiter. From the simple reminder 'You've forgotten the table napkins' to a full debriefing on how he served at table on a busy Saturday night, the head waiter is providing feedback that will shape the candidate's future performance to the desired goal of being the perfect waiter. If the candidate is working towards an NVQ, this formative assessment will also give him an indication of when he will be ready for a formal end-assessment.

2. A candidate working towards an NVQ in Learning and Development is receiving formative assessments from a number of different people. These are her supervisor, who sits in on some of her training sessions; other trainers in her area of work, with whom she discusses various aspects of work on a regular basis; and the clients she is training, who are asked to evaluate each session they attend. These are in addition to the more formal formative assessment that the candidate has received from her assessor, who has made a diagnostic observation visit to one of the candidate's sessions.

3. A candidate for the NVQ in Cleaning and Support Services has regular tutorial times with his assessor following workplace observation and the completion of written tasks. The assessor uses progress review forms to identify how the candidate is doing, what he has achieved, and how, and where and how he needs to improve. This is a formal method of providing formative assessment. As the candidate achieves different areas of his units, the various performance criteria, scope and knowledge are marked off on his assessment record.

4. A mature candidate in Information Technology, attending an open-learning workshop, is very nervous about the idea of 'being assessed'. She is given

regular constructive formative feedback on her progress, with a chance to discuss how she can improve. The candidate is given encouragement to decide when she feels ready for a formal assessment.

Table 2.1 Formative and summative assessment

	Characteristics	**Purpose**
Formative assessment	Ongoing continuous feedback for improvement	To diagnose and plan
Summative assessment	Final summing up of achievements at a particular point in time	To describe and accredit

Summative assessment

Summative assessment represents a formal 'summing up' of the candidate's achievement on completion of a particular piece of work. In the case of NVQs or mini-awards, this would be at the completion of each unit. An assessor will make a final judgement on the whole of a unit after making a series of formative assessments. The results of this assessment will be recorded to stand as a statement of the candidate's competence at the time of the summative assessment. Other examples of summative assessment include:

- end-of-year/end-of-course examinations;
- end-of-unit tests for craft certificates;
- the final grade given to completed projects or assignments.

METHODS OF ASSESSMENT

There are a number of assessment methods commonly used in NVQs. This next section considers six of these methods in detail: observation, oral and written testing, simulation, professional discussion and the assessment of prior competence.

Observation: assessing practical competence

This is the main method by which competence should be assessed, and involves observation of performance and/or examination of an end product. Many people in work will have been involved in informal assessment of performance by observing and making judgements about how effectively someone is doing his or her job. Instructors or trainers will be used to watching how an individual trainee learns or behaves, and will make mental notes on areas of strength and areas where they may need help. However, assessors of NVQs and small awards or mini-awards do need to be able to observe and record their findings in some permanent way.

The person carrying out an observation may find it useful to follow these key points on the observation process:

- Be clear about what is being assessed and the processes involved.
- Ensure that the candidate has been involved in the planning process, and clearly understands what will happen.
- Use a checklist as an aide-mémoire (reminder) if it helps.
- If not familiar with the place of assessment, try to visit it beforehand.
- Try to give the candidate some control over the conditions, eg ask their opinion on the best place for the assessor to stand or sit and, if feasible, respect their wishes.
- Keep out of the eye line of the person being assessed.
- If the candidate's work involves interacting with clients or colleagues, keep out of his or her eye line and workspace.
- Avoid becoming involved in the assessment process.
- When clients are involved, make sure the candidate knows that the needs of the client should take precedence over the needs of the observing assessor (though hopefully by following occupational standards, both will be accommodated!).
- Make sure that anyone else involved is informed and reassured about the presence of an observer.
- Ensure that, whenever possible, there is time after the observation to give immediate feedback and discuss what has been observed.
- Make sure that all external visitors to the candidate's workplace (eg assessors, verifiers) comply with the requirements of the organization and with relevant legislation, such as the Health and Safety at Work Act.

Example 1: Observation in the workplace

If we look at the floor plan in Figure 2.2, a number of factors would influence where the observer performing the assessment was positioned. If the assessor worked in the salon, both clients and staff would be used to their presence and hence the assessor might choose to stand right next to the candidate when he or she was working with the client (A1). If the assessor came from outside the salon, his or her presence would be more noticeable and this would have to be taken into account. If the observation was assessing general client care and service, then the assessor could sit on a seat in the waiting area (B1) and arrange that the candidate always worked in the position nearest to the shop window, ie the position with client number 1. The assessor could then move to have a final look at the finished 'product' once the client's hair had been styled. However, if the observer were assessing competence in perming hair, then close observation of techniques and procedures used would be essential.

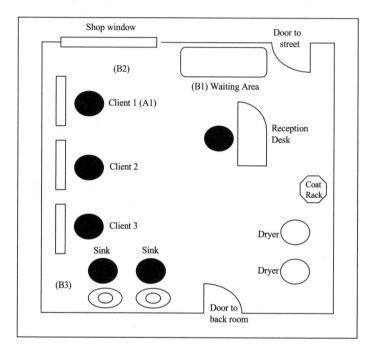

Figure 2.2   Floor plan of a hairdressing salon

In this case, the assessor would need to be next to the candidate and, in that situation, would obviously need to decide where he or she could stand to cause the minimum disruption. There, it would probably be a good idea to ensure that the candidate was not working in the client number 2 position. This would be because the assessor would have to stand in the small space between two sets of clients. Possibly position (B3) might be the least intrusive, with the candidate working with client 3.

Example 2: Observation of a group working

An assessor for NVQs in Learning and Development or Management might have to conduct an observation of someone conducting a meeting, giving a presentation or running a training session. The danger here is that the assessor will find him- or herself physically in the middle of the group, and this is bound to affect the 'normality' of the situation.

Apart from the general points already mentioned, the following may be helpful:

- It could be useful to arrive before the group meets and place a chair at the back of the room outside the area where the participants will be sitting.
- Apart from greeting people briefly and pleasantly if appropriate, minimize conversation with members of the client group, otherwise the 'dynamics' of the group may be altered.
- Avoid too much eye contact.
- Use a method of recording the observation that is as unobtrusive as possible. Rustling papers can prove disruptive in a quiet environment where people are concentrating on what is being discussed, and the use of video recorders can unnerve those who are not used to them.

In certain circumstances, it may be inappropriate or impossible for the assessor to be present when a candidate is performing a task or carrying out a procedure. In such cases, the use of witness statements, audiotape or videotape (*if accompanied by an explanation*) is admissible evidence.

Questioning: assessing knowledge and understanding

The use of questions, either oral or written, is the main method for establishing whether the candidate has knowledge and understanding across a range of contexts and contingencies. This is vital, as without knowing what exactly he or she is doing, why, and what the possible alternatives are, there is little possibility that an individual will be able to transfer any skill from one situation to another. Instead of the desired highly skilled and flexible workforce, we might end up with a nation of robots.

There are limits to what an observation can tell the assessor about how much someone actually understands about what they are doing. An observation is at a particular time and place, in a particular environment, under a particular set of circumstances. For example, the assessor could observe someone using a computer. That observation might not enable him or her to tell whether that person could cope if a fault appeared in the program, or if the person were working on a different type of computer, or if the person were working in a busy environment under a lot of time pressure. Well-constructed and relevant questioning can find out this information from the candidate.

We can often infer a good deal about what someone knows by what they do or what they produce. For example, if we observe someone involved in child care instructing small children to wash their hands before eating, we can infer that the child care assistant knows at least one basic rule of hygiene. Similarly, if we are shown a completed press article produced by a journalist, we might infer that he or she knows how to structure information and spell words correctly. However, we must be very careful in inferring just how much someone knows from what we see that person do. In the first example, the child care assistant could just be copying what he has seen others do, without any knowledge of the reason why he is doing it, in which case he probably has no concept of the 'idea' of hygiene and hence would not be able to transfer this rule across to another situation. In the case of the journalist, we may be satisfied that she has produced the article herself, but has she used a dictionary to help her spell? Has she used a standard format to structure her article? In both examples, the key to assessing whether someone really knows something needs to be taken from the level of qualification. At lower levels, the definition of knowledge could just involve 'has information about', and the understanding required could be very limited. At higher levels, the definition of knowledge should include a deeper understanding of the knowledge aspects related to the element, plus a broader ability to transfer and make connections between ideas and practice.

In Chapter 9 there is a more detailed explanation of how different testing methods suit particular work contexts. However, it is obviously important to choose questioning methods appropriate to the activity being tested. The next section will consider the different types of oral questions and written tests that can be used.

Open and closed questions

Broadly speaking, questions can be divided into the categories of 'open' or 'closed' types that have distinctive features and functions. Open questions, associated with prompt words such as 'How?' and 'Why?', offer the opportunity for candidates to respond fully and in their own words. Closed questions are associated with phrases such as 'Do you think. . .?', where the candidate can only respond with 'Yes' or 'No', and with prompt words such as 'What?' and 'Where?', when the candidate is required to respond with specific factual information.

Choosing the right type of question

Assessors need to be clear on why they are asking a particular question and predetermine what answer or answers will be acceptable. At levels 1 or 2, it is likely that questions will be simple and closed, because specific factual knowledge is being tested. For example, at NVQ level 2 in Construction, a candidate might be asked to give five examples of construction work that would need to be protected against the weather while other work was being finished. The assessor will know the range of acceptable answers and will accept any five of these answers from the candidate. Some more open questions may also be appropriate, eg asking the candidate 'why?' he or she is using a particular process or piece of equipment. It is likely that the answers to these questions would be fairly short and simple.

Function	Example
Set at ease	'Would you like a coffee?' 'What sort of journey have you had?'
Ask for general information	'What were your responsibilities as. . .?' 'What have you been doing in the past year?'
Ask for specific information	'What is your name?' 'How do you save data on a disk?' 'Precisely what does that entail?'
Ask for further information	'Could you tell me some more about that?' 'Can you give me some more details?'
Identify agreement or disagreement	'Do you think he acted correctly?' 'Did you agree with the way she dealt with that situation?'
Ask the reason or justification	'Can you tell me why you used that particular technique?' 'Why is ice put in the glass before pouring the drink?'
Ask for opinions, ideas	'What do you think of this product?' 'Do you believe in positive discrimination?'

Figure 2.3   Different functions of questions

At level 5, the question and answer process will inevitably become far more complex. For example, a strategic manager (the candidate in this case) may need to show that he or she has an effective management style. The candidate's underpinning knowledge of why he or she has adopted a particular style over others could be assessed by a variety of techniques. These could include questioning and discussion between the assessor, the candidate and the candidate's colleagues, and demonstration by the candidate that his or her chosen style results in positive outcomes from the candidate's staff, and the achievement of corporate objectives. This would be far more useful and valid than asking the candidate to write a report or assignment such as 'Compare and contrast different management styles, with special reference to your work situation'.

Oral questioning

In most work contexts the testing of knowledge and understanding in NVQs will normally be oral rather than written. For example, a supervisor will ask an employee why the employee has increased the speed of a manufacturing process, how the employee intends to use the new floor polisher in a safe manner, or what the ratio of sand and cement is to water for a particular mix of concrete. Every occupation has its underpinning knowledge and understanding requirements, which are used as a basis for assessment. In order to carry out an oral assessment, assessors need a thorough knowledge of the standards, so that they are able to ask appropriate questions. The A&V awards each have their own set of questions that candidates can use for self-assessment, that assessors can use as a basis for checking knowledge and understanding.

An assessor could ask questions at appropriate times during an observation or set aside a separate time after the observation to ask *all* necessary questions together. Alternatively, the assessor may choose to question knowledge and understanding across the range or scope of the element once all performance evidence has been assessed. The assessor and candidate through discussion should make these decisions. The knowledge evidence needs to be judged in the light of all other evidence the assessor has gained about the candidate's competence.

Questioning skills

- *Putting the candidate at ease.* It goes without saying that the candidate is likely to be nervous, and the assessor needs to be sensitive to this. The more confident that candidates feel, the more likely it is that they will be able to give a true representation of what they really know. It usually helps if candidates actually know what the procedure will be, know that they can ask for a question to be repeated and know that they can take their time answering.
- *Ensuring the language is at the right level and can be understood.* Be clear as to what is being tested, and avoid using over-complex language if this is not necessary. Be aware of what the candidate's normal range of vocabulary is likely to be and take that into account when phrasing questions. Distinguish between essential technical jargon that the candidate will need in his or her vocational area, and inessential use of over-sophisticated vocabulary.

- *Not asking leading questions.* Assessors should be careful not to use questions that could lead the candidate by giving him or her a clue to the right answer. They should also be aware of any preferences or opinions they might hold that could affect the way they ask questions. It is just as easy to lead the candidate by the tone or inflection of voice or by some facial expression or body movement. One assessor we know would automatically purse her lips and lean forward slightly if the answer she was getting was incorrect. However difficult it may be, a neutral but pleasant expression is the ideal!

'Your client seemed a bit uncomfortable, didn't she?'
'Don't you think you should have cleaned the floor before the woodwork?'
'Why would you say UVPC was better than wood?'

Figure 2.4 Examples of leading questions

Written testing

There are a number of different types of written testing used within NVQs, and the choice of the appropriate test format depends entirely on what level and complexity of knowledge and understanding need to be demonstrated. The main ones are as follows:

Yes/no or true/false response A statement is followed by either a yes/no or true/false response to be ticked or circled.

Example: A larch tree is an evergreen: true/false.

Objective tests (multiple choice) A question is asked followed by several alternatives, out of which one must be selected.

Example: A chronological filing system is one in which files are arranged according to:
(a) geographical area;
(b) initial letter of surname;
(c) date received;
(d) reference number.

Gapped statements A statement or longer piece of text has a space or spaces left for the candidate to complete.

Example: Foods that are high in fibre include. . . and. . .

NB: Sometimes the candidate is free to write any appropriate word and sometimes the word or words can be selected from a given list.

Short answer tests   A series of questions may be set that require answers of a few words or a few lines.

Example: Explain briefly how a colour correction filler works.

Essays   Set topics, usually with a defined number of words, often involving research through reading and including the structuring and development of ideas.

Example: Discuss how different learning theories can be used in planning training programmes.

Reports   Reports should be on a set subject with clearly defined objectives based on practical research, to be laid out with headings, following a conventional report structure.

Example: Write a report on the procedures for employee appraisal within your organization with recommendations for improvement.

Assignments/projects   Assignments or projects should be on set topics, usually entailing some practical research and a written explanation and analysis of what has been discovered.

Example: Choose one specific client group in the community, eg young mothers, pensioners, etc. Find out what services are provided for them and their opinion of these services. Compare local to national provision. Present your information using both written and visual means.

Difficulties in assessing knowledge and understanding

All the methods we have set out can test knowledge from a simple to a sophisticated level. However, it is evident that those requiring more complex responses will be far more useful in establishing whether candidates actually understand and can apply the knowledge they are demonstrating.

The more complex the activity, the greater the possibility of showing competence against a number of different elements and the more opportunity there is for demonstration of other skills. The assignment given in the example above would also enable candidates to demonstrate a variety of key skills, including *communication, working with others* and *problem solving*. If it involved analysis of data, they could also cover *application of number*, and if the results were produced using a computer, then *information technology* would also be covered. However, there are a number of difficulties in the assessment of knowledge and understanding:

- The assessor primarily has to make a decision on how much knowledge and understanding can be inferred from what a candidate is doing or what he or she has produced. Sometimes this is straightforward, particularly if the assessor is in regular contact with the candidate and has observed the candidate a number of times covering a range of situations and contexts. However, sometimes this could be misleading – for example, assuming that a trainer being assessed 'knows' about different learning theories because he or she has used a number of different teaching methods.

- The more complex methods of testing knowledge such as by setting essays also pose difficulties for the assessor. The material produced by the candidate is more individualized and there are far more in the way of information and ideas to disentangle, hence the demands on the assessor to have very clear ideas of what will or will not be acceptable and what is or is not relevant are far greater. Such assessments have obvious advantages, in that candidates have a full opportunity to express themselves if appropriate. However, the potential for subjective and unfair assessments can be considerable. It is important that the assessor has a clear marking scheme *prior* to the assessment being distributed to candidates, and that he or she knows the marking criteria (spelling, whether references are required, complexity of analysis required according to level, number of expected examples, etc). This helps the assessor to mark objectively.

- There is sometimes a problem in being sure about the depth of knowledge to be demonstrated, and it can be difficult to gauge this from reading the standards. There is no easy answer here, and guidance should be obtained by consulting with external and internal verifiers and ensuring consistency of understanding and practice between assessors through standardization and moderation exercises. However, it is possible to form some idea of the depth of knowledge required by referring to the description of the level of qualification. For example, NVQ level 1 refers *to routine and predictable work activities*, whereas level 5 refers to a *significant range of fundamental principles across a wide and often unpredictable range of contexts.*

- The limitations of testing knowledge in relation to specific elements rather than covering larger inter-related areas are also seen as problematic by some assessors. This can be an issue if knowledge at all levels is treated in an over-simplistic way. However, it is important to remember here that a substantial piece of evidence could be cross-referenced so that it provides proof of knowledge and understanding across a whole group of elements. It is up to those advising and assessing to help candidates to realize this holistic approach where appropriate.

An increasing number of NVQs contain externally marked assignments, where the candidate answers a set question in a specific timescale in particular circumstances. There are a variety of ways in which this is done. Often, candidates are given the topic in advance, so they can research and prepare for a given number of days. The assessment may then be done at the centre in supervised conditions, perhaps with the use of the notes they have made. Centre-marked assignments are another option. The purpose of this type of assessment is to encourage candidates to be able to show their knowledge, rather than trying to catch them out.

Setting tests and devising marking criteria for projects and assignments

This book cannot go into the necessary depth required on this broad subject, but readers are referred to the texts in the Suggested Reading section. The crucial factors are that test questions need to be designed so that candidates cannot guess the answers, and that assessors need to share with candidates the basis on which they will be marking assignments *prior* to issuing the project and assignment briefs.

Simulation

The amount and nature of simulation for each NVQ is laid down by each NTO. Awarding bodies will give further advice on when and how simulation is to be used. It is a method that enables a very limited set of circumstances to be demonstrated. These are usually connected with particular areas such as dealing with a fire, or a spill of hazardous chemicals, that might never arise in normal work practice, but where the candidate must know how to respond.

Professional discussion

Professional discussion gives the candidate an opportunity to talk through, demonstrate, show and clarify aspects of his or her work that still need evidencing and/or for which other types of assessment are less appropriate. The assessor will plan carefully for professional discussion in order to obtain the clarification needed. The plan needs to be agreed with the candidate. Professional discussion should be workplace based and candidate led. This also gives opportunities for the offering and protection of confidentiality, security and the demonstration of complex competences.

The professional discussion must be recorded in some way. One method of recording is by audiotape, as this unobtrusive method gives proof of the discussion. The assessor can take photographic evidence to augment the taped conversations. There is no necessity to transcribe the conversation. If the camera can record date and time, this is often a more acceptable form of recording 'live' evidence than is videotape, and sits well alongside an indexed audiotape. Video, ideally using a small digital recorder, can be used where it would cause no disruption to normal work activity and where the candidate feels it would aid his or her demonstration of competence. The third method of recording, taking down the discussion verbatim, is the most difficult and least appropriate to do, as the assessor is less able to give full attention to the candidate, and the discussion can become stilted owing to the need to write everything down.

Assessment of prior competence and experience

Candidates who have a good grasp of the standards and have been working to them for some time will, particularly at NVQ level 3 and above, benefit from using evidence from prior achievements. They can identify recent and relevant evidence within their workplace, and ask for witness statements to back this up. The professional discussion can be used to explore the candidates' background and how this affects their current practice. There will still need to be at least one assessment of current competence by the assessor.

SUMMARY

This chapter should have helped you with the following:

- the terminology used in assessment;
- different types of assessment;
- different methods of assessment;
- skills in observation and questioning;
- problems in assessing knowledge and understanding.

3

The Processes Involved in Assessing NVQs and Short/Mini-awards

This chapter looks briefly at how the assessor and verifier awards fit into the overall Learning and Development framework and then focuses on the four stages involved in the assessment process, concluding with an explanation of key processes related to NVQ assessment. The Learning and Development standards are included in Appendix 1 for reference.

ASSESSMENT AS PART OF THE TRAINING CYCLE

There are a number of different models for the training process, but although the terms may vary from one model to another, the essential stages are similar in nature. They all have the following features:

- *initial review* – diagnosis of what the candidate already knows or can do, compared with what he or she needs to demonstrate and learn;
- *design of learning* – decisions are made and agreements are reached on what the outcomes of learning should be, how the learning is to take place, what methods and resources will be used, and what timescale is appropriate; this is done with regard to cost-effectiveness, health and safety, and equal opportunities practice;

- *implementation* – the learning programme is put into practice;
- *assessment* – the results of learning are assessed, usually throughout the programme, as well as at the end;
- *evaluation and quality assurance* – a variety of techniques are used to gain quantitative and qualitative information on the overall effectiveness of the process, from candidate satisfaction to the meeting of organizational targets.

The Learning and Development standards follow this sequence, which is seen as a cycle, since the results of evaluation and quality assurance feed back into the process to affect work with the same or the next candidate as they progress through or start their programme.

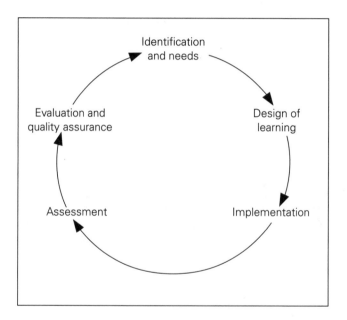

Figure 3.1 The training cycle

NVQs focus on the assessment of what people can competently do, and what they currently know and understand, rather than how they acquired that skill or knowledge. The Learning and Development standards related to assessment have been used to create units that are known as the Assessor and Verifier (A&V) awards. These are explained in greater detail in Part 2. Depending on your job role, you will need one or more of the following:

- A1 is for those undertaking assessments of workplace performance and knowledge using a range of methods to carry out the assessment.

- A2 is for those carrying out assessment of skills in the workplace, using observation and questioning.
- V1 is for those verifying the assessment procedures within an organization.
- V2 is for those who are externally verifying assessment procedures. It is taken by external verifiers, who are appointed to their jobs by awarding bodies. It is not covered in depth in this book. It is run by the awarding bodies for their own verifiers, though the standards themselves have been included for reference.

THE NVQ ASSESSMENT PROCESS

Most people involved in assessment will be covering the assessment process as a natural part of their work, and the four stages involved will be familiar to them, although they may not have identified these stages explicitly. This process is reflected in the Assessor Awards for A1 and A2, which require evidence that all these stages of assessment are adequately covered. In this chapter we look in detail at what each stage actually involves.

Stage 1	Stage 2a	Stage 2b	Stage 3	Stage 4
Planning for assessment with candidate	Reviewing performance and knowledge evidence	Judging all evidence against agreed standards	Recording decisions and giving feedback	Contributing to quality assurance processes

Figure 3.2 Stages of the assessment process

Stage 1: Planning for assessment

In order to make sure that assessment is absolutely fair, no candidate should ever have a 'surprise' assessment. He or she should always have been involved in the planning stage and will have agreed, following training and in advance of any assessment activity, to the assessment process for each unit being taken. Obviously, the level of negotiation between candidate and assessor may vary according to the ability of the candidate and the context in which the planning takes place. Candidates who are new to the NVQ system at any level will initially need a lot of help and guidance. However, they can still be given opportunities to make their own suggestions and choices without putting them in a situation where they feel overwhelmed. Many candidates with various learning difficulties successfully complete NVQs. Again, with support and guidance they will be able to contribute ideas towards the way their assessment can be achieved.

The assessor and the candidate will meet to plan how and when a unit or units are going to be assessed, and by whom. Once the candidate understands the requirements of each whole unit and the associated assessment process, planning meetings should not be too lengthy. Ideally, the candidate will have regular assessment by his or her assessor through workplace observations, followed by feedback and review of the assessment plan. The assessor who is not in regular face-to-face contact with the candidate, perhaps because much of the assessment is being done by a vocational observational assessor (A2), needs to keep in touch by other means such as telephone, e-mail or letter in order to monitor progression of the planned assessment programme.

Although planning for assessment will normally take place on an individual basis, there may be times where the planning takes place with a whole group of candidates. This might be because a specific activity, eg an assignment, that covers a number of competences has been set up. Whatever way the planning meeting takes place, both candidate(s) and assessor need to be clear on a number of key areas:

- *What* competences will be assessed?
- *Who* will be involved in the assessment?
- *When* will they be assessed?
- *Where* will they be assessed?
- *How* will they be assessed?
- *How* will achievement be recorded and confirmed to the candidate?
- *When* will feedback be given?
- *How* will feedback be given?
- *Are* there plans which cover the assessment process for each complete unit?

Examples of planning for assessment:

- A candidate working towards an NVQ in Motor Vehicle Repair is assessed at the garage where he works. As the assessor in this case is the owner of the garage, and they see each other every day, assessment takes place on a fairly continuous basis, with the previously agreed assessment plans for each relevant unit being continuously reviewed and updated. They also take advantage of spontaneous opportunities for assessment – for example, the candidate suddenly gets a job that will give him the chance to demonstrate a particular competence and so arranges, more or less on the spot, to be observed and assessed. The key to this type of planning is that both need to be clear initially about the competences required for each unit of the NVQ and about the methods and opportunities available for assessment. They also need to establish a procedure for taking advantage of these 'spontaneous' opportunities that may occur.

- An external assessor is assessing a candidate working towards an NVQ in Beauty. They have a meeting to review the unit assessment plan, at which they discuss what competences still need to be demonstrated and decide that some competences related to nail care have not yet been covered. The candidate gives the assessor a number of dates and times when she will be carrying out a full nail treatment and they arrange a convenient time for the assessor to come and observe her. They then check whether any other competences could be covered at the same time and decide that the candidate could also be assessed on some elements related to health and safety and customer care. Assessment plans are revised for these units.
- Catering students at a local college working in a training restaurant have a group meeting with their tutor before they go into a lunchtime session where they are serving at table. They agree on a number of competences that they should have the opportunity to demonstrate during that time and which can be observed and assessed. After the session, the assessor works with the students to update their individual unit assessment plans and record their progress, in their online portfolios.
- A candidate wishing to submit evidence for APL towards an NVQ in Photographic Processing has a first meeting with her primary assessor. During this meeting the assessor acts as adviser and helps the candidate to match her past experience against the requirements of the NVQ and works with her to identify what evidence will be appropriate to support her claim. They agree on an appropriate timescale and possible date for assessment. During this planning meeting the assessor explains his role, making a clear differentiation between the advising process and the assessment process that follows it. The assessor draws up plans for each NVQ unit, which identifies what APL evidence will be brought forward and what additional methods of assessment will be used to complete the unit assessment. He agrees to make arrangements for assessing the evidence at their next meeting.
- Students who are candidates on a Key Skills programme are given an assignment by a tutor during a classroom session. The briefing for this assignment gives instructions on what needs to be presented for assessment, when it should be presented and the criteria against which it will be assessed.

In all these cases, the details of what will be assessed, any action that needs to be taken prior to assessment and any changes to the already agreed assessment process for individual units should be recorded on the assessment plan. Assessment plans and planning are covered in more detail in Parts 2 and 3 of the book.

Identifying relevant evidence

It is common to refer to the activities and products that the candidate will perform or produce to demonstrate competence as 'assessment evidence'. 'Evidence' is usually associated with a legal situation where information, videotape or audio recordings, documents, artefacts or witness testimonies are produced to prove the defendant innocent or guilty. And just as the police and lawyers work to collect and review the evidence in order to make their case for the prosecution or defence, so assessors need to understand and gather knowledge about the candidate's competence.

The onus is not necessarily on the candidate to provide everything, just as it is not up to the defendant to prepare his or her own case. It is true that sometimes defendants represent themselves, and confident and experienced candidates are likely to need less support from assessors. Defendants are assumed innocent until proved guilty; similarly, it would be wrong to suggest that candidates for NVQs are guilty of incompetence until they provide the evidence to prove themselves innocent; they have not yet demonstrated competence. NVQ candidates in work have often been performing competently for some time, but have not had the opportunity to prove they are working to national standards. However, it is useful to bear in mind the rigorous examination given to legal evidence to assess its worth. For example, a legal witness has to be credible and consistent in his or her testimony and able to stand up to cross-examination. Legal documents always need the signatures of reputable persons to confirm that they are truthful and accurate. Circumstantial evidence, along the lines of 'Well, he was there at the time, so he must have done it!', is not sufficient, and there must be other hard evidence to back it up. Similarly, witnesses to a candidate's competence must be credible and link their statements to the required evidence standards.

Just as in a court of law, the evidence produced must clearly relate to the identified required performance criteria or knowledge and be able to stand up to rigorous examination. Hence the candidate and assessor should be clear not only about what they have to do or produce which will provide evidence, but also about what *quality* of evidence is needed. During the planning for assessment they must discuss:

- what types of evidence are appropriate to meet the specified performance criteria;
- what knowledge can be assessed either through performance, questioning or discussion;
- arrangements for the assessments;
- how the evidence will be assessed;
- who needs to be involved;
- what documentation and procedures need to be used.

Candidates should also have discussed the best way to go about identifying opportunities for proving competence. In many cases they will have been helped to produce an action plan that identifies what they need to do prior to assessment. Examples of action plans can be found in Chapter 9.

Access to assessment

Assessors must be mindful during the planning process that individuals are not excluded from access to assessment. Figure 3.3 gives some indications of the kinds of barriers that might prevent individuals from gaining access to assessment.

There are many different kinds of problems that people might face, and all assessors will have their own examples. Here are a few from our own experience and the measures taken to combat them:

- A candidate in information technology who developed arthritis. A special keyboard overlay was obtained for the computer, which helped her to hit the keys accurately.
- A candidate in residential care who could only work on the night shift. An assessor was found who was prepared to conduct an assessment observation during this time.
- A candidate in an engineering firm, whose first language was Somali, spoke good enough English to carry out his job. However, he needed help in understanding the details of how he was to be assessed. An interpreter was found who attended the planning interviews to make sure that he was able to understand and discuss anything that was necessary.
- A young girl who had been in care since she was a child was placed on a Foundation Modern Apprenticeship programme working with animals. She was given a good deal of encouragement and a very slow and gentle introduction to the process of assessment by giving her feedback on an informal basis. When her supervisor was certain she had a good chance of being successful, she suggested that the girl be assessed against one unit of the qualification. Success in this increased the girl's confidence and she was soon able to be assessed against other units.
- A candidate wanting to be assessed for commercial harvesting was told by the assessor where he worked that he would have to wait until June to harvest the strawberries. This is because candidates had *always* been assessed harvesting strawberries. When it was pointed out that it was just as possible to assess the candidate harvesting another type of crop, the assessor realized that the candidate could be assessed almost straight away – harvesting winter broccoli!

These are some situations that could affect the candidate's access to assessment

Physical
If the practical assessments were to take place on the first floor of a building with no wheelchair access, a candidate in a wheelchair would be unable to be assessed.

Chronological
If assessments always took place after 3.30 pm, parents who had to collect children from school could be disadvantaged.

Linguistic
If a candidate's mother tongue was not English, he or she could have difficulty understanding the assessment requirements.

Social
Candidates lacking in confidence could be too nervous to submit themselves for assessment.

Intellectual
A candidate with learning difficulties could need much more support before he or she was ready for assessment.

Resource-based
If the resources, eg equipment needed for assessment, were not readily available, candidates would not have the opportunity to be assessed.

Cultural
Candidates who were asked to perform activities that were unfamiliar to them, or were abhorrent to them (eg not being allowed to wear the shawl, if a Muslim woman), might have to refuse assessment opportunities.

Gender-related
Candidates might be prevented from doing tasks that the workplace felt were not appropriate even though they were quite capable of doing them, eg male teaching assistant, female forklift truck driver.

Figure 3.3   Examples of barriers to access to assessment

Stage 2: Reviewing performance and knowledge evidence

The assessor will determine the evidence of competence by using at least four different assessment methods. Some methods of assessment for different types of evidence are shown in bold below:

- *performance evidence:* by **observation of the candidate** carrying out a task or procedure that occurs naturally in a work situation, or carrying out a practical activity such as taking part in a discussion or performing an experiment in a science laboratory;
- *differing sources of product evidence:* by **examination of products** such as memos or reports, assignments, or photographs produced by candidates or of items they have made such as a cake, a painted wall or a repaired tyre;
- *evidence from prior experience:* by **reviewing and checking statements from credible witnesses** for relevant evidence from past activities and situations in which the witness has seen the candidate carrying out work to national standards, and presenting previously assessed work from prior activities;
- *evidence elicited through professional discussion:* by **having a planned, recorded discussion** in which the candidate is prompted to talk through his or her role and activities, and shows supporting evidence (ideally captured on video) to validate the knowledge and performance claims being made;
- *knowledge evidence:* by **questioning or testing** candidates to confirm that they understand the principles underlying their actions, the consequences of acting in certain ways, and what they might do in different circumstances.

Evidence can be:

- *direct* – it reflects their own work, ie the candidate either performs it or produces it him- or herself;
- *indirect* – other people or other sources provide the information about the candidate's work, ie a third party confirms that the candidate is competent in a particular area. This 'third party' can be a person such as an employer or a customer who produces a statement about the candidate, or it can be a qualification that the candidate has achieved.

Once the evidence is reviewed, the assessor needs to decide whether it proves that the candidate has met the required elements and performance criteria, and scope and/or range of the unit. When making these judgements, the assessor needs to take a number of different things into account. The terms used in Figure 3.4 are the most common – and the most important – terms involved in assessment judgements. All these conditions need to be met by the evidence provided.

Let us look more closely at each of these terms in turn.

Validity

- *The assessment process and the evidence required should be appropriate to what is being assessed.*

The candidate is COMPETENT	NOT (YET) COMPETENT
The evidence is	
Valid	Not valid
Reliable	Not reliable
Sufficient	Not sufficient
Authentic	Not authentic
Current	Not current

Figure 3.4 Terms used in assessment judgements

It would not be valid to assess whether a cook could bake a cake by asking him to draw a picture of one. Nor would it be valid to assess whether a gardener could plant bulbs by watching her sow seeds. Valid assessment implies that the method (or methods) used are the ones most likely to give an accurate picture of that individual's competence within a particular area.

Old-fashioned methods of assessing a student's ability in a foreign language often lacked validity. It is amazing to think that a person's ability to communicate in French was formerly tested by having the person complete a series of written grammatical exercises rather than on whether they could actually speak and be understood!

Validity has a particular significance in NVQs because what is being assessed is the evidence presented. If the evidence is not valid, ie it is not an appropriate means of demonstrating competence, then the candidate will have to be reassessed using different, or additional and more relevant, evidence. What is important to grasp is that no evidence is automatically valid or not valid. It is the candidate's interpretation of that evidence and how he or she justifies its relevance that makes it valid.

For example, a photograph of the candidate and another person could be presented as evidence. By itself that photograph has no meaning. However, if the candidate says, 'This is a photograph that appeared in my firm's newsletter showing me receiving a prize for apprentice of the year', the photograph takes on a meaning and becomes valid evidence (as long as the candidate can prove that it is true). This is why explanatory statements related to any documentary evidence presented are important, as they can give the reasons why the candidate believes a particular piece of evidence to be valid.

Another possibility for invalidity would be if a candidate provided witness statements from colleagues who were also candidates for the same NVQ award. If these colleagues were very experienced in the area, but had just never converted that experience into a qualification, their evidence might well be valid. If, however, they did not really have the depth of knowledge or experience to warrant acting as a witness, the validity of the evidence could be questioned.

Reliability and fairness

- *The judgement confirms that the candidate's performance will be of a consistent standard in a range of different contexts.*
- *The same assessor would make the same judgement about the candidate on a number of different occasions.*
- *Other assessors would make the same judgement about the candidate.*

Another way in which subjective judgements can cloud the objectivity of an assessment is in the 'halo and horns' effect whereby a candidate is considered 'good' or 'poor' by the assessor, and all evidence is judged on that basis, as opposed to being judged on its own merit. Probably the most effective safeguard that can operate here is the assessor's own awareness of where he or she might be biased or have personal preferences, plus a strict adherence to the requirements of the elements being assessed. Reliability and fairness are closely linked. Candidates must have confidence that they will be treated fairly by assessors, that they are not going to have a harsher assessment from one assessor than from another, and that another candidate is not going to be assessed more leniently than themselves. Candidates are entitled to feel confident that they will be treated fairly when working towards NVQs.

This means that the assessment process should be free from bias or discrimination. Candidates need to be sure that they will not be discriminated against because of some personal prejudice of the assessor. Most of us would probably agree that many people interpret guidelines differently, or consider some aspects of work more important than others. These can all affect our judgements and make them different from candidate to candidate, and different from the judgement of someone else doing the same assessment. Hence measures that ensure consistency are essential if we are to be fair to the candidate. Consistency in NVQs is also essential for employers or educational institutions, which will be asked to accept that the standards give a clear and accurate picture of how someone can perform in employment or in preparation for progression to other education or training programme. These bodies will need to rely on the quality and consistency of the judgements being made.

Sufficiency

- *The evidence is enough to prove competence.*

In our experience, *insufficient evidence* does not usually mean too little evidence but *too little evidence of a relevant kind*. This can result from a 'shopping trolley' approach to the assessment, whereby all sorts of documentary items are collected in the vague hope that they will provide something of substance. If being assessed is to be meaningful for the candidate, an essential part of the process is the thought required in discussing his or her own performance, in assessing his or her own strengths and areas for development and in working out what he or she needs to do, make or explain to demonstrate competence appropriately. Without this disciplined identification and selection, candidates will remain unaware of what it is that they do or know that enables them to perform a particular work role. Here are some examples of evidence that is not sufficient:

- a letter (as a witness statement) from an employer that does not refer to the specific competences performed by the candidate;
- a document without any explanation as to its relevance;
- a practical activity with no questioning to show that the candidate has the underpinning knowledge;
- evidence of competent performance on just one occasion, or within a very limited time span.

Authenticity

- *The evidence is genuine and has been produced by the candidate.*

Some traditional assessment methods, such as end-of-term examinations, provide safeguards to ensure that candidates cannot cheat. An independent invigilator watches them while they write their answers, there are rules about what items of equipment can be present and strict rules of secrecy about what they might be required to answer.

NVQs are practically based, so sound assessment is crucial. Inaccurately assessing a candidate as competent say in construction or motor vehicle repair could have potentially fatal consequences. Independent assessment has been introduced for many NVQs as a double check on the assessment process. An experienced assessor, independent of the candidate, who may never meet them, assesses some of the candidate's evidence. Some awarding bodies stipulate exactly what the independent assessor will assess; others request that 'a significant part' of the candidates' work is independently assessed. The knowledge requirements for NVQ units can be assessed by a variety of methods such as externally assessed written tests or assignments, or, more usually, by written answers to pre-set questions marked by a centre assessor. In all these cases the assessor should apply the appropriate safeguards against copying or cheating.

Determining whether performance evidence is genuine will obviously be reasonably straightforward if the assessor is observing the candidate actually doing something at work. However, the assessor has to be sure that any end product presented by the candidate as 'one I made earlier' really has been produced by that candidate. Assessors will also have to decide whether witness statements are genuine, and will need to look at original certificates where the candidate is claiming that he or she has prior qualifications. Documents included by candidates may not be their own work. This may be innocent, in that the candidate has not realized that he or she needs to show understanding and application of policy, rather than including the copy of the company document. Assessors do need to be on the lookout for documentation that purports to come from the candidate, but has differences in spelling, sentence structure and/or grammar from other documentation that they know is the candidate's own work.

Currency

- *The evidence can prove that the candidate is up to date on current methods and equipment required in the appropriate occupational area.*

Some examples of where this issue could occur:

- A candidate for NVQ in Business Administration worked in an office 4 years ago. Would this provide evidence that she could work in an office now?
- A candidate for NVQ in Learning and Development has a teaching qualification obtained in 1983. Would this provide evidence that he could work in a training environment now?
- A candidate for an NVQ in aircraft maintenance engineering has been off work for two years because of an accident. Would she still be up to date with the skills and technology required?

There are no hard and fast rules here. Obviously, every occupational area is different, and some change far more quickly than others. However, as a general rule, areas that deal primarily with people can use evidence that dates back over a greater number of years than occupational areas where rapid changes in technology are likely to make skills obsolete – even those acquired only a few years before.

Safety

There are two possible meanings here. The first, and *intended*, meaning is in the sense of:

- *The assessor can safely say that the candidate is competent.*

In other words, the assessor considers, after taking into account all the evidence, that the candidate's practice is sound. Assessors must ensure that their judgements are 'safe' by ensuring that the candidate can maintain the standard consistently over time.

The second interpretation is to do with health and safety. Although this is not the intended meaning of 'safe assessment', it is true that:

- *The activities carried out by candidates must be done in accordance with the Health and Safety at Work (HASAW) Act.*

Under the HASAW Act, employees have a responsibility to report unsafe practice or equipment, and to conform to the workplace health and safety policy. The only time an assessor or internal verifier should interfere with an assessment is if health and safety are compromised in any way. The assessment should be stopped and appropriate action taken with the relevant people.

Stage 3: Recording assessment decisions and giving feedback

The majority of assessments contain some subjective judgement, particularly when assessment is of more complex skills or knowledge. There are times when a subjective judgement is appropriate – for example, when a candidate asks for a personal opinion of a particular idea, process or product. However, in general, so that assessment is fair, reliable and to national standards, it is important that safeguards are in place to make the summative assessments of NVQs as objective as possible. This can be a problem when working to performance criteria, where language such as 'relevant' and 'appropriate' is frequently used. The nature of the language may lead to subjective interpretations that reflect the personal bias of the assessor, and hence are neither fair to the candidate nor a reliable indicator of a 'national' standard.

One major safeguard is for the assessor to check out his or her own interpretation of such woolly terms with other assessors and internal and external verifiers. Some consensus might then arise to curb any subjective excesses. Standardization events should be held on a regular basis by internal verifiers so that assessors can check their interpretations of the standards, and of their candidates' achievement of standards, against the judgements of others using the same materials as a baseline.

Again, standardization events will help assessors become aware of biased judgements, and internal verifier sampling will also help to identify any judgements made without good basis in fact.

Unfair discrimination

NVQs emphasize good equal opportunities practice, based on equal access to assessment irrespective of age, gender, religion, ethnic group, disability or geographical location. In our experience there is still a lack of awareness regarding the circumstances in which discrimination can occur. Knowledge about equal opportunities issues, the policies of their own organizations and the legislation that exists can help those involved in assessment to become more aware of what they need to address. One of the most powerful means of preventing unfair discrimination is to make an open-minded examination of one's own beliefs and prejudices and how they may affect one's judgement. The subject of equal opportunities is far too extensive to be covered here in any detail; however, here are some examples of how discrimination might affect judgement:

- an assessor being prejudiced against someone because he or she thinks the person is too young to have the required skills, rather than objectively viewing the evidence;
- an assessor in child care being particularly hard on a male candidate because the assessor does not think that this is 'man's work', so wants to discourage him;
- an assessor undervaluing the practical skills demonstrated by a candidate whose first language is Urdu, because the candidate's command of English is not perfect;
- an assessor being over-generous in his or her assessment of a candidate who is a wheelchair user.

Some of these may strike a chord in the reader. If not, dig deeper. The majority of us have at least one significant prejudice that could affect our ability to assess fairly!

NVQs have been accused of being a mechanical system of collecting pieces of paper, ticking boxes and recording results, and, like any system, they can be treated in a minimalist fashion. However, if the stages of the assessment process are covered sensitively and with integrity, NVQs can provide a good developmental experience for candidates. One stage that is fundamental in any development process is the feedback stage, at which candidates are given specific information about what they have achieved or not achieved. Candidates are also given the opportunity to discuss this fully with the assessor. An important word in this context is 'discuss'. This implies a two-way process of identifying strengths and areas for improvement, with the assessor using a considerable amount of skill in involving the candidate in analysing what, if anything, needs to be improved before the next assessment.

The skill of giving constructive and helpful feedback is at the heart of successful assessment. If this skill is used, candidates will not just be clear on what they have achieved, but will be clear too on what they need to do to develop or maintain performance. They will also be motivated by the feedback to try to improve on their performance. Some examples of situations where feedback could be given (and received) are from an assessor to a candidate who has just had a workplace observation, by an APL adviser discussing a candidate's first attempt at a portfolio of evidence, or to an assessor by their internal verifier. In every case, badly delivered feedback can destroy confidence and trust. This is particularly important if the candidate has not been able to demonstrate competence or achievement and might be tempted to give up and not try again. It is crucial to be sensitive to how the other person is responding to what is being said.

It is crucial to record the results of any assessment, formative or summative, at the time of assessment so that:

- there is a clear record of what the candidate has already achieved;
- the assessment plan is kept updated, showing what else if anything needs to be done prior to final assessment;
- records can be accessed by internal or external verifiers at any point during the candidate's progress for quality assurance purposes;
- there is proof that the assessment process is meeting requirements agreed between the centre and the awarding body, and which follow the national standards for assessment and verification.

Stage 4: Contributing to quality assurance processes

Verification is the main quality assurance process associated with NVQs, and will be carried out within the centre by internal verifiers, and on behalf of the awarding body by external verifiers.

Internal verification is at the heart of good competence-based assessment practice, as internal verifiers can ensure through their monitoring and support of assessors and their assessment decisions that there is a degree of trust in the process. This trust in the way in which decisions are being made should lead to assessors taking the lead in being able to confirm the competence of a candidate without requiring that candidate to provide unnecessary documentary evidence in a portfolio. The assessment that the assessor makes in the workplace, either through observation of practice, *or through the observation and inspection of documents and processes and systems in situ,* should encourage the

1. Let candidates have the first say
Give them the chance to say why they think they have been given their particular result. If they are competent, build on their understanding. If they haven't achieved competence, it is possible they will know why, and this will help them to 'own' the feedback they receive.

2. Give praise before criticism
Most people will find it difficult to try to improve if they feel they are a failure. By focusing first on their strengths and then helping them to recognize their weaker areas, you can give candidates enough confidence to deal with anything that needs to be improved.

3. Limit what you cover
Don't try to cover everything. Focus on two or three key areas for development.

4. Be specific, not vague
Try to avoid general comments that don't help the candidate to identify the issue. It's not very useful to say to someone, 'Your writing isn't very good.' It is much more useful to say, 'It was difficult to read what you had written, because your writing is rather small and you crowded all your information together without leaving any spaces between the different sections.'

5. Concentrate on things that can be changed
For feedback to be useful it must allow for the possibility of improvement. If there are intrinsic or extrinsic factors that you know cannot be changed, the feedback relating to this is a waste of time. It is far more useful to concentrate on what can be changed.

6. Give the candidate time to think and respond
Successful feedback involves a 'dialogue' between two individuals committed to improvement. If you have given the candidate a new perspective on some aspect of competence, it could take some time for him or her to absorb. Only when the candidate has absorbed it and then responded can the planning for improvements take place.

7. Keep to the standards
As assessor/adviser, you must distinguish between when the candidate has done something different from how you would do it but has still met the standards and when he or she has not performed to the required level of competence. You might draw the candidate's attention to this difference, but be clear as to whether it is acceptable in relation to the standards or not.

8. Make sure the candidate understands
Think of the language you are using and ensure that the level and tone are right.

9. Listen to how the feedback is received
Be aware of how the candidate is reacting to your feedback. Look for non-verbal cues that he or she is confused or doesn't agree.

10. End on a positive note
End the feedback session agreeing some positive action that can be taken to address any areas for development that have been identified. End with some encouragement as well!

Figure 3.5 Points to consider when giving feedback

development of diverse naturally occurring relevant evidence from candidates, with the minimum of documentation.

Assessors will contribute to the internal verification process by recording and submitting data (such as dates of assessment, achievement records for candidates, and assessment plans and feedback records). They will also be required to participate in standardization of assessment exercises, and be observed making workplace observations and engaging in professional discussions. Likewise, the internal verifiers will have to provide information to the external verifiers, who will check that they are carrying out sampling assessment practice properly, and that the centre is conforming to the NVQ Code of Practice. Most organizations will also have their own quality assurance processes, which may require the identification of yet more data, such as enrolment data, and the recording of the destinations of candidates once they have completed their NVQs.

Quality assurance is a vital part of any national qualifications system. All national assessment systems need to ensure that everyone involved in the assessment of candidates is assessing correctly, working to agreed procedures and to an agreed standard of performance. This cannot just be left on trust to individual assessors but needs to be part of a strict monitoring framework that covers not only the individual assessor, but also all the assessment within an organization and, finally, all the assessment nationally.

SUMMARY

This chapter should have helped you with the following:

- key stages in the (NVQ) assessment process;
- key terms in the assessment process;
- planning assessment and identifying evidence;
- reviewing performance and knowledge evidence;
- terms involved in making assessment judgements;
- recording assessment decisions and giving feedback;
- unfair discrimination;
- contributing to quality assurance processes.

4

The People: Key Roles in the NVQ Assessment Process

This chapter looks at the roles carried out by those involved in assessment and verification, and the requirements they need to meet for the assessment strategy in order to assess or verify the awards. Any system is only as good as the people who take part in it, and the quality of skills and knowledge of those involved are key factors in making the system credible and worthwhile.

ASSESSMENT SYSTEMS

Most assessment systems, including those for traditional qualifications, have a number of common aspects (Figure 4.1).

These are followed by those who play key roles within the process of assessment. They: 1) specify what areas of knowledge and skill are to be assessed; 2) identify the circumstances in which assessment should take place; 3) decide the parameters for achievement or non-achievement; and 4) follow procedures for carrying out and documenting the assessment, and reporting the outcomes.

KEY ROLES IN ASSESSMENT AND VERIFICATION

There are a number of participants within the NVQ assessment system. These are:

WHAT?   Skills/knowledge/understanding to be assessed

WHO?   Candidate/assessor/internal verifier/witness/independent assessor/ external verifier

WHEN?   Appropriate place(s), time(s) and opportunity(ies) for assessment

HOW?

- Criteria for achievement/non-achievement (in some systems pass/fail)
- Procedures for informing the candidate of requirements
- Procedures for assessment
- Procedures for informing the candidate of results of assessment
- Procedures for documenting the results of assessment
- Procedures for monitoring the assessment's accuracy
- Procedures for reporting outcomes

Figure 4.1   Components of an assessment system

- *The candidate* being assessed, who will demonstrate his or her knowledge and competence in the workplace, typically via performance, the answering of questions, products, and witness statements. Most NVQs now have a clear emphasis on achieving the award through real work situations, with only very strictly stipulated simulation allowed. The candidate will therefore be in a role that enables him or her to achieve the NVQ units required without recourse to simulation or 'manufactured' situations. Candidates following Learning and Development awards that include Assessor and Verifier units should note that simulation is not permitted in these awards.
- *The primary assessor (A1)*, who identifies clearly, with a candidate, what needs to be assessed, determines the most appropriate range of methods to use in assessment and then negotiates assessment opportunities with the candidate and others who may be involved. After reviewing and judging a range of evidence, the primary assessor ensures that the results of assessments are properly fed back to, and recorded for, the candidate. Primary assessors sign off complete units for candidates. They ensure that all materials and methods used follow good equal opportunities and health and safety practices. They also contribute to, and participate in, the organization's quality assurance system. Primary assessors can be working towards their A1 award themselves, in which case a qualified assessor must countersign all their decisions.
- *The observational assessor (A2)*, who is involved in workplace observation and questioning. This is a narrower role than A1, in that the assessor uses just a couple of assessment methods, and may never sign off complete units

for candidates. Observational assessors can be working towards their A2 awards themselves, in which case a qualified assessor must countersign all their decisions.

- *The independent assessor (A1)*, who is able to give a second dimension to quality assurance at the assessment stage. Not all NVQs require an independent assessor, but this is laid down in the assessment strategy prescribed by ENTO for Learning and Development NVQs and mini-awards. The independent assessor does not necessarily meet the candidate, but does assess a substantive part of the candidate's evidence. For a full NVQ, this is normally a unit. In the case of the A1 award, this is most often one of the minimum of four complete agreed and reviewed assessment plans covering a complete NVQ unit that will be produced by the candidate-assessor. The independent assessor must be a fully qualified assessor, in both occupational area (eg Manufacturing, or Learning and Development) and assessment (ie D33, A1).

- *The internal verifier (V1)*, who ensures that the assessment roles are being carried out correctly within the organization, and who manages internal quality assurance for the award. This is done by drawing up sampling plans, and internally verifying that the judgements made by assessors (including independent assessors) are correct and to the national standards. Internal verifiers will also monitor and support assessors, liaise with a number of stakeholders such as the awarding body via the external verifier, and produce reports on the assessment and verification practice for which they are responsible. They may undertake the administrative tasks required (see below) if there are no separate administrative staff.

- *Centre administrative staff*, who deal with the processing of registrations and certification for the award. They are likely to be involved in the production and distribution of materials related to the awards. They are sometimes the contact person between the centre and the awarding body, and may, on behalf of the internal verifier(s), keep the awarding body updated regarding centre changes.

- *The external verifier (V2)*, who monitors the internal verification and assessment procedures for a centre. The awarding body for the qualification appoints occupationally competent external verifiers to centres. External verifiers sample a range of judgements made by verifiers and assessors, recording their findings and distributing them to the centre, the awarding body and the lead verifiers. Lead verifiers monitor the performance of external verifiers both qualitatively and quantitatively, as do the awarding body's administrators, who receive copies of, and analysis of, their centres' reports.

ROLES AND RESPONSIBILITIES OF PARTICIPANTS IN THE PROCESS

The candidate role

In traditional programmes the candidate has often been someone that assessment is 'done to' without the candidate's previous experience being taken into account and without the opportunity for him or her to be involved in the process. So, in the past, an examination question for telephone engineers on a day-release course might have been along the lines of 'Write an essay of between 600 and 800 words on the history of the telephone'. In a situation such as this, the activities and products required of the candidate were not dependent on who they were or what they had done; everyone, irrespective of background or experience, had to answer the same questions. Nor was the evidence the most valid means of showing that they were capable of doing the job of telephone engineer. However, over the past 40 years, much has been done by many awarding bodies to introduce methods of assessment that are more closely related to real-life work requirements and also to place more responsibility on candidates to reflect on their performance and identify areas for improvement.

The role that NVQ candidates take is one of active involvement in their own assessment. This starts at the planning stage, where candidates are encouraged by the assessor to identify their current skills and past experience, and to negotiate the evidence for competence and knowledge, and the methods for their assessment. Most candidates will need advice and sometimes a substantial amount of guidance and support from an adviser or assessor. Candidates who are familiar with the procedures and evidence required for each unit could, after the initial assessment planning and agreement of unit assessment plans, proceed without any further input or advice from another source, other than liaising with their assessor(s)for the necessary observations and assessments.

The (primary) assessor role (A1)

Assessors are expected to assess, using at least four methods of assessment, the knowledge and performance of their candidate through encouraging him or her to identify a range of relevant types of evidence as possible for each NVQ unit. These types of evidence could include, among others:

- the candidate's oral or written answers to questions;
- observation of the candidate's practice;
- products from the candidate, such as a logbook or an item he or she has made, endorsed video or photographic evidence;

- a report from the candidate or from the candidate's peers;
- judgements from others, including work-based assessors and witnesses;
- evidence from the candidate's prior experience;
- simulation, in a narrow range of instances (but none in the Assessor and Verifier (A&V) awards).

The need for this range of evidence is based on the idea that competence often entails more complex skills, particularly at the higher levels. The majority of jobs involve a range of situations that need different skills and abilities. In more complex jobs, many different competences are required, not all of which can be assessed through direct observation of performance. Take, for example, a situation where a manager in a local government office is working towards a management NVQ. It would be both expensive and time-consuming to observe the manager undertaking all aspects of the manager's role as determined by the standards. Even if much observation was undertaken, not all aspects of that role might actually be observed in day-to-day activities. However, the primary assessor could use other sources of evidence to ensure that this manager was competent, including testimonies from line managers and colleagues, examples of written communications such as memos and letters, minutes of meetings chaired by the candidate, and talking to work colleagues. This variety of sources of evidence will give a more rounded picture of the candidate's knowledge, ability and skills, and enable a sound judgement to be made.

The primary assessor needs to be able to assess all these different sources of evidence with rigour, using the performance criteria as the determining factor for competence.

The observational assessor role (A2)

The most straightforward way of finding out whether someone is competent in a particular area of work is to watch him or her actually doing it. A hairdresser might write essays about hair styling, produce testimonials from satisfied clients and previous employers and display photographs of hairstyles he or she has created. This will all be valuable evidence, allowing the assessor to infer that the candidate has knowledge, understanding and certain skill levels. However, the surest way of establishing whether the candidate can perform with competence is for an occupationally qualified assessor to observe him or her in a hairdressing salon, styling and cutting people's hair. The other way an assessor might assess directly is by looking at something the candidate has produced – for example, a cupboard made by a joiner, or a Web site produced by a media candidate. The assessor will then, through questioning and discussion, find out how well the candidate understands the consequences and context of that activity.

Someone using a piece of equipment:	Forester using a chainsaw, Hairdresser using a hairdryer
Someone performing a service:	Kitchen assistant following rules, Care assistant giving a bed bath, Waiter/ress serving a drink
Someone making a product:	Joiner making a cupboard, Student producing an action plan
Someone showing a particular skill:	Candidate working well as part of a team, Manager negotiating with their staff
Someone carrying out procedures:	Gas service engineer observing safety procedures

Figure 4.2 Examples of performance evidence

The independent assessor role

Not all NVQs require independent assessment, but this role is mandatory for the assessment of A&V awards. The independent assessor must be fully qualified as an assessor, and be familiar with the candidate's vocational area. His or her role is to bring some external quality control into the internal assessment process. The independent assessor assesses a substantial component of the candidate's work, which may be predetermined by the awarding body. This could be a complete unit within a full NVQ.

For the A1 and A2 awards, the independent assessor will usually assess one assessment plan for one candidate for a complete unit, with its reviews and explanation. This will be one of the plans that the candidate-assessor has developed and worked through with their own candidate. It will show how the candidate-assessor has supplied his or her own vocational candidate. However, the independent assessor could assess any other part of the unit. It is better *not* to use an internal verifier as the independent assessor as this has been found to lead to confusion (QCA report 2004).

The internal verifier role

The role of the internal verifier is *to conduct internal quality assurance of the assessment process (V1)*. This role is crucial to the quality assurance of NVQs and of the centres offering them. Its importance is reflected in the fact that those undertaking it are expected to be working at level 4 – in other words, holding managerial rather than supervisory status. Within all but the smallest organizations there will probably be more than one person acting in the internal verifier role. In all organizations delivering Learning and Development awards, including the A&V awards, the internal verifier will need to co-ordinate the activities of the assessors, including those who may be independent or peripatetic assessors. Internal verifiers may need to manage across a number of related vocational awards areas. The internal verifier is responsible for implementing an internal verification strategy. This must be in compliance with the Learning and Development Assessment Strategy, the assessment strategy for the vocational NVQs being taken by candidates, and the NVQ Code of Conduct, and with regard to the JAB Guidance and other documents produced by the QCA (see the list of further reading at the end of the book). They ensure that both candidates and assessors show evidence of consistent occupational competence and that assessments and quality assurance conform to national standards. It is the internal verifier's role to see that this happens by ensuring that:

- there is regular contact with the awarding body;
- assessors have sufficient occupational competence and have records of recent occupational and assessment updating;
- assessors are given all the necessary help and information they need to be able to assess effectively and efficiently;
- the quality of assessments is monitored and standardized on a regular basis;
- they are available to answer queries if assessors experience difficulties.

Large centres will have an *internal verifier co-ordinator* who allocates the workloads of all the internal verifiers, and is the point of contact with the awarding body and the organizations quality manager. An internal verifier co-ordinator will usually act as the team leader for the internal verifiers, ensuring that information and procedures are fully consistent within the internal verification team.

The external verifier role (V2)

Monitoring of quality and consistency at a national level is done through a network of external verifiers appointed through awarding bodies. External verifiers are experienced senior practitioners in the broad area of the standards they verify. Their role is to approve centres that wish to offer NVQs, approve the schemes that approved centres wish to implement, and be assured of the quality of assessment and internal verification procedures – in other words, that they are being carried out to the national standards both for assessment and verification and for the vocational area. *The vocational area for those assessing A&V units is Learning and Development.* As the external verifier is the main link between the centre and the awarding body, he or she should also be the person who can give answers to queries from centres – for example, on the acceptability

---

Example 1
Two assessors, A and B, and one internal verifier, C: good, because the IV is able to standardize and is separate from the assessment process.

Example 2
Assessors B and C are both qualified internal verifiers. B internally verifies the work of A and C. C verifies the work of B: not as good, as B and C could get complacent, and are also standardizing with each other. There is no standardization between the results of A, B and C.

Example 3
Ten assessors, one IV: good, because the IV can standardize across the 10 assessors, but problematical if anything happens to the IV. A second IV is needed for security and support with decision making.

Example 4
Eight assessors, all qualified as IVs, who work in pairs, verifying each other's assessments. Poor: too many variables of assessment practice, too little independence. Better to select a couple to run the IV, leaving the rest to assess, and build in regular standardization events between the assessors and the IVs. The role of IVC could rotate each year.

Figure 4.3   Examples of poor and improved allocation of internal verifiers and assessors within a centre

of certain evidence or on the interpretation of certain performance criteria. Usually, external verifiers are line-managed by their awarding body's administrative managers, and are supported by their regional lead verifier for their occupational area.

Different combinations of roles

Within the roles identified, there are clearly opportunities for different combinations and variations, depending on the nature and size of the organization. For example, an assessor may be a work-based assessor for one candidate, a primary assessor for a second and an independent assessor for a third. He or she might also be qualified as, or be working towards being, an internal verifier and have his or her own allocation of assessors to support and mentor. One combination of roles that must *never* occur is that of assessor and internal verifier with the *same* candidate. That does not prevent someone from acting as an assessor with one candidate and then as an internal verifier with a candidate who has been assessed by another assessor. Centres need to ensure they have enough staff to avoid compromising quality through internal verifiers having too little time to carry out their role.

Case study 1

A candidate working in a large engineering firm is advised and assessed by her immediate supervisor, acting in the role of primary assessor. The supervisor from another section, a qualified (D33/A1) assessor, acts as the independent assessor, assessing one of the candidate's NVQ units. The senior manager of the section is the internal verifier, monitoring the process and procedures of the assessment, and arranging for external verification.

Case study 2

A candidate who is a student on an NVQ in the Learning and Development programme put on by his local college is given an assignment by his tutor on learning styles and teaching methods. Before the assignment, he has been given an individual interview with his tutor, who has acted in the informal role of adviser, giving him help on how to approach the assignment. This tutor will act as primary assessor observing the candidate work as a trainer in his organization. The same tutor will also assess the candidate's work diary and the assignment produced, and will use the feedback given by the supervisor and other staff working in the organization to make a final assessment judgement. The programme co-ordinator will take on the role of the internal verifier, and will arrange for a significant activity carried out by the candidate to be assessed by an experienced independent assessor. The work will be selected by the candidate in telephone consultation with the independent assessor, and sent to the independent assessor via the internal mail.

Case study 3

A candidate with considerable management experience, working within a local authority, wishes to claim APL towards an NVQ in management for what she has achieved in the past. One of the local authority training officers, acting in the role of adviser, discusses with her what evidence would be appropriate. Another training officer acts in the assessor's role and makes an assessment judgement on the evidence. The line manager from another section who has achieved D34, and has demonstrated to the external verifier that he has upgraded his skills to V1, acts as internal verifier.

Case study 4

A candidate is trained by her line manager in assessment practices. The organization is small, and has joined with two other small organizations to form a consortium, which has registered as an approved centre. Her primary (A1) and independent assessors are from the other two organizations within the consortium, as is the internal assessor. The primary assessor does one work-based observation, but her line manager acts as the observational assessor for all other work-based assessments. This arrangement allows these small centres to run their own awards in a cost-effective and efficient way, without compromising quality or integrity. The activities of all these four staff are managed by a fifth, who takes on the role of internal verifier co-ordinator.

SKILLS WITH PEOPLE

Candidates have a variety of different needs, and the centre's assessment systems and staff need to be flexible enough to take account of these. The fairness and reliability of assessment judgements can be affected by not taking into account the characteristics of candidates and the situation in which they are working. Let us look at four different candidates and briefly identify considerations in the approach to the assessment of the individual candidates.

NVQ level 1: Amenity Horticulture

The candidate has learning difficulties and a tendency to get worked up under pressure. However, he has shown a real aptitude for gardening and could hold down a regular job.

Here, the assessor should try to be friendly and natural, making as little of the assessment process as possible in order to give the candidate the best chance of demonstrating his ability.

NVQ level 3: Registered Care Manager Award

The candidate has worked for a number of years in voluntary service, where she held a position of some responsibility. She then began work in a hospice, where she is dealing with patients sympathetically and effectively.

Here, the assessor would need to be aware of the sensitivity of the situation and might consider it appropriate to take the lead from the candidate about how to carry out the assessment. In particular, the feelings of the patients would need to be a major consideration. Witness statements from qualified staff who work closely with the candidate and understand the demands of the NVQ could form a large part of the evidence.

NVQ level 2: Sport and Recreation

The candidate is 17 years old and working towards this qualification at college. The primary assessor will probably be a college lecturer and might also be using the assessment to monitor the student's general progress and response to the programme.

In this situation, the assessor would probably liaise with assessors based in the candidate's workplace to compare judgements on progress in order that the feedback to the student could be as informed as possible.

NVQ level 5: Learning and Development

The candidate is a senior manager in a local authority. At this level, the assessor would expect that the candidate should be well used to pressure and responsibility.

The main consideration would be to help the candidate to utilize all opportunities for work-based assessment, ensure that the assessments do not take more of the candidate's time than is strictly necessary, and to use APL and recorded professional discussion as a way of cutting down paperwork for the candidate.

Anyone assessing or advising on NVQs will be dealing with a variety of different candidates, all with their own characteristics and particular needs, who are not just having assessment 'done' to them but who are encouraged to take an active part in the assessment process. Some candidates may find this easy and, after the initial briefing, will get the idea of what is required and be quite happy to take a proactive role. Many candidates will not find it so easy and will view their possible involvement with suspicion, and perhaps trepidation. The adviser or assessor may find this a tricky situation and may be tempted to take one of two extreme approaches. One approach might be to abdicate all responsibility and tell the candidate it is up to him or her to plan for assessment and for the collection of evidence. The other approach might be to take on a highly directive role and tell the candidate exactly what he or she thinks the candidate should do. In some cases, the failure of the first approach might lead the adviser or assessor to fall back on the second. The skill for the adviser or assessor is to do neither, but to weigh up the amount of support and guidance appropriate for each candidate at each stage in working towards the qualification. Some hints on this:

- Ensure that the candidate has a clear overview of the whole qualification and of each unit.
- With inexperienced candidates, help them to make choices by the use of structured alternatives, eg 'Would you prefer. . . or. . .?'
- Always give candidates the opportunity to make suggestions.
- Avoid immediately rejecting suggestions made by candidates.
- Explore disagreements rather than impose your own point of view.
- Be clear yourself on what you can negotiate and what you cannot.
- Make it clear to candidates what can or cannot be negotiated.

- If candidates refuse to accept your advice, consider this carefully.
- If you are blocking their right to choose, think again.
- If, by not taking your advice, they will not produce appropriate evidence, make this clear.
- Avoid giving too much responsibility too soon, as this could inhibit some candidates by making them feel overwhelmed.
- Note down on the assessment plan everything that has been agreed and discussed. If there are activities the candidate needs to do that are pre-assessment (eg training), these can go on to an action plan.

OCCUPATIONAL COMPETENCE AND CONTINUOUS PROFESSIONAL DEVELOPMENT

Using the standards for development

As important as consistency in assessment and verification practice is the need to maintain a developmental rather than a mechanistic approach to competence. In other words, there is scope for the standards to be used in holistic, questioning and creative ways rather than in prescriptive, narrow and fragmented ways of assessing competence outcomes. This often needs addressing by the organizations using standards, as much as by individuals. When the Training and Development Lead Body first published the standards in 1992, the potential benefits of an imaginative approach to their use were given in the Executive Summary. These were:

- as a basis for job descriptions;
- to identify training needs;
- to develop training programmes;
- as benchmarks for development;
- as a basis for assessment.

The summary also stated the expectation that the National Standards for Training and Development would 'enable employers to design, promote and support the kinds of personal and professional development cultures they needed to create and sustain amongst their workforces' by:

- providing basic requirement specifications that could be used in the purchase of training services;
- indicating the kinds of criteria that should be used to evaluate the progress and outcomes of training programmes;
- acting as an operational guide to the design, development and delivery of training programmes;

- underpinning the introduction and use of innovative, non-traditional training methods, systems and materials;
- incorporating best practice in human resource development planning and strategy design approaches;
- providing ways of reaping the obvious benefits of workplace assessment to specific standards by qualified assessors and verifiers.

The new Learning and Development Awards (2002) assist this process in extending the range of mini-awards, and linking them into some nationally identified areas for development, such as the management of basic skills in the workplace.

One of the biggest problems faced by individual candidates and by organizations that are helping their staff to acquire relevant awards is that of discovering either that job roles are narrower than the standards require, or that practices and procedures do not tally with the standards' requirements. The discovery of 'gaps' can lead to resentment towards a competence-based approach to outcomes measurement, and create problems with trust and motivation. This can be a particular problem where there are difficulties in agreeing on the interpretation of standards, where staff feel threatened (eg does lack of demonstrated competence equal *in*competence?), and where tried and tested procedures are being changed to accommodate the new approaches. Sensitive and informed advice from assessors and advisors can help candidates to select appropriate standards and qualifications that candidates will find achievable. Discussion related to implementation of standards can in itself be a powerful tool for staff development as current job roles, programme content and assessment techniques are compared with those that would be required. It is not uncommon to find that a complete programme of staff development takes place, sometimes deriving from the discovery that assessment practices across departments differ significantly. Standards can also be used successfully to give a fair framework to traditional, process-based programmes.

All assessors and internal and external verifiers already qualified with or still working towards the D units have a first-hand opportunity to use the A&V standards for updating. They now need to show how their practice has moved to incorporate the demands of the new standards for assessment and verification. The new Learning and Development Standards also give the opportunity for assessors and verifiers to develop their own (Learning and Development) vocational background through matching their current skills and knowledge to the new standards, and perhaps take new qualifications themselves as a result.

Continuous professional development (CPD)

Assessors and internal verifiers are now expected to show that they are competent both in their vocational area, such as Financial Services or Travel and Tourism, but also that they have occupational competence in the area of Learning and Development. This occupational competence needs regular analysis against the requirements of the industry. Internal verifiers and assessors need to show how they are monitoring their competence, and how they plan to maintain the currency of their skill and knowledge.

Each NTO or standards-setting body has within its assessment strategy clear requirements for the professional updating of its participating assessors and verifiers. For the assessors and verifiers of A&V awards, this is a minimum of two updating activities per year. These should be planned and clearly auditable. Examples might be attending training sessions on new qualifications, participating in regional standardization exercises, joining in (auditable) sustained online discussions about aspects of internal verification or assessment, or producing and delivering induction programmes for assessors or internal verifiers.

Most awarding bodies and professional organizations run regular updating events for their centres. Assessors and internal verifiers can also update by utilizing the information provided on the ENTO's Web site.

SUMMARY

This chapter should have helped you with the following:

- the NVQ assessment system;
- understanding the roles of candidates, assessors, verifiers and administrative staff;
- people skills;
- continuous professional development;
- using the standards for organizational and personal development.

Part 2

The Requirements of the
Standards

Introduction: Assessment and Verification in Practice: How to Use the Step-by-Step Guides

Part 2 explains the requirements of the performance criteria in A1, A2 and V1. This section is for anyone interested in understanding the good-practice requirements for the assessment of work-based competence, whether via an NVQ or via other competence-based programmes. Assessors and verifiers qualified to D32/33 and D34 will need to familiarize themselves with the requirements of the new standards and demonstrate that they are operating to the requirements of A1, A2 and V1 as appropriate. Those readers who are familiar with the previous D Unit awards will recognize the welcome simplification in the language of the standards that had been hoped for by so many. In fact, it was the complicated language of the former standards that led us to write the first edition of this book in 1994. Since the standards and supporting materials published by ENTO are now so much more straightforward, the step-by-step guides in this edition are somewhat different from those in previous editions of this book.

We will refer you to the text elsewhere in the book where necessary, and also to relevant materials on ENTO's Web site. Each awarding body offering the award has developed its own support materials and documentation, usually available at a very small cost, and you will find it helpful to have this material, as well as any additional documentation that is provided by the centre with which you are taking the award.

One of the new pieces of information is the Learning and Development Assessment Strategy that has been developed by ENTO (see Appendix 3). Each NTO has developed an assessment strategy for its NVQs, and these need to be read in conjunction with the standards for that NVQ. An assessor who was assessing, say, a candidate-assessor for A2 whose candidates were taking NVQs in Engineering, and who was going to cover the work-based assessment as well as the overall unit advice and assessment for A1, would need to meet the requirements of both the Engineering NTO Assessment Strategy and the Learning and Development NTO Assessment Strategy.

A final point

If you are a candidate-assessor or candidate-verifier, remember that your own primary assessor, workplace assessor, independent assessor and internal verifier should be modelling the competences in the awards. The process you follow with them should be the same as the process they help you to follow with your own candidates or assessors. They should be encouraging you to discuss and ask for clarification on any points that confuse you, and providing you with clear assessment plans that cover each whole unit being taken. *Make sure they do their job!*

THE STANDARDS

The Learning and Development Awards are made up of sets of related standards grouped into units. A unit is a definable task or number of related tasks. The task is subdivided into sub-tasks or elements. Each element comprises a number of performance criteria, which specify what is required for competent performance. The scope of the unit is defined, ie the range of circumstances in which it could be carried out, as well as the underpinning knowledge that every candidate should have in order to perform the tasks with understanding. A1, A2 and V1 each consist of a single unit with four elements. Low-unit-number qualifications are known as mini-awards. Most full NVQs have around 10 units. The A1 & A2 awards are part of the NVQ in Learning and Development at level 3. The V1 award is part of the NVQ in Learning and Development at level 4.

A1 AND A2

A1 and A2 now include aspects of the former D36 (Advise and support candidates to identify prior achievement) within them.

Assessors of full units need to take A1, which is the broader of the two awards. It covers the common assessment processes of:

- planning unit assessment, to include a range of methods, with candidates;
- assessing a range of evidence sources covering competent performance, knowledge and understanding;
- giving feedback and recording results;
- providing records that contribute to the quality assurance system.

A1 has developed from the previous D33, in that planning has an increased focus, and there is an explicit link into the standardization and quality assurance processes of the centre. The requirements to have three assessment plans with reviews for *complete* NVQ units for a minimum of two different candidates, three assessments and two assessment records also reflect a desire that candidate-assessors show evidence of supporting candidates over a sustained period of time. The range of methods for assessment that assessor-candidates need to show competence in using has also been increased to cover a minimum of four. The introduction of recorded professional discussion (preferably by video) gives the opportunity for the candidate to offer more evidence orally and for the assessor to be able to check a wider range of the candidate's knowledge. If video or timed and dated photographs are used, there is no necessity to include materials in the portfolio that can be seen on the images.

A2 will be needed by assessors who are involved only in workplace observation and the assessment of knowledge relating to the observed activities.

It should be extremely difficult for candidates who are not bona fide assessors to get the awards, just as it should be impossible for candidates to get the award if their internal verification system is not geared to continuous sampling and standardization, of which they are an integral part.

David Morgan, Director of Marketing and Communications at ENTO, has said:

> Without an effective, robust internal quality assurance process that is underpinned by a clear strategy, assessor-candidates will be unable to achieve the new A1 unit, as this unit requires the assessor-candidate to contribute to the internal quality process or internal standardisation. . . Therefore for those organisations whose Internal Verification practice is that of end loading portfolios of evidence then their assessor-candidates will not be able to achieve their award. (*The Learning Network for Assessors and Verifiers Newsletter*, issue 2, Spring/Summer 2002)

V1

V1 is now an award at level 4. The internal verifier (IV) is therefore deemed to be operating in a 'managerial' or co-ordinating role, liaising with internal and

A1 assessors who assess only their vocational subject can do any of the following:	A1 assessors who assess A1/2 and/or V1 in addition to, or as part of, their vocational subject, can do any of the following:
• Train others in the background to the assessment of their particular vocational award, eg horticulture, care, retail, construction • Assess competence in the workplace related to their specific vocational area • Assess knowledge related to workplace competence related to their specific vocational area • Assess evidence from a variety of other sources, including simulation, professional discussion, evidence from prior achievements or experience • Act as independent assessors	• Train others in the background to the assessment of their particular vocational award, eg horticulture, care, retail, construction, learning and development • Induct others to the requirements of the new assessor awards • Assess competence in the workplace for their own vocational area plus the A&V awards • Assess knowledge related to workplace competence for their own vocational competence and for the A&V awards • Assess evidence from a variety of other sources, including simulation, professional discussion, evidence from prior achievements or experience • Act as independent assessors
A1 assessors assessing only their subject and *no* A&V awards need:	**A1 assessors assessing their vocational subject *plus* the A&V awards need:**
• A vocational qualification in their subject area at level 3 or • Experience in their subject area that gives them competence at level 3 • A1 • To meet the assessment strategy requirements of their subject-related NTO	• A vocational qualification in their subject area at least at level 3 or • Experience in their subject area that gives them competence at level 3 • A vocational qualification in the area of Learning and Development at least at level 3 *or* experience in the Learning and Development area that gives them competence at least at level 3, eg NVQ 3 in Learning and Development, Cert Ed, PGCE, C&G 7306/7 or equivalent • A1/A2/V1 according to job role • To meet the assessment strategy requirements of their subject-related NTO • To meet the assessment strategy requirements of ENTO

Figure I2.1 Roles and qualifications and experience needed by A1 assessors

external quality assurance staff. There is a greater emphasis on the analysis and evaluation of the findings from verification activities.

IVs who are currently qualified to D34 must provide updating evidence that they themselves understand and meet the new criteria for IVs at level 4. This updating means that IVs need to be fully familiar not only with D32/33, but also A1 and A2. They themselves need to be operating at A1 in order to carry out V1.2 satisfactorily.

IVs now need to demonstrate explicit monitoring of observation of assessors, and checking of the decisions of assessors across candidates over time. The IV role has always been the key to a centre's quality, and the new V1 awards enhance this.

5

Guide to Unit A1: Assess Candidates Using a Range of Methods

The standards in this unit are followed by those who:

- assess candidates against agreed standards of competence using a range of assessment methods;
- give candidates feedback on their assessment decisions; and
- contribute to the internal quality assurance process of the centre.

This covers all primary assessors and independent assessors, whatever their vocational competence. It is crucial that assessors for A1, A2 and V1 are exemplary in their practice of the standards, as candidate-assessors and candidate-verifiers are likely to use them as role models.

A1 assessors do not necessarily assess performance themselves, as they may use the judgements of others (eg A2 assessors or witnesses). They will, however, assess the whole of the evidence provided by candidates for complete units.

Giving candidates an overview of how they can demonstrate competence and knowledge for a clear set of tasks, as defined in an NVQ unit, helps them to progress clearly and swiftly to achievement.

A1 has four elements:

- develop and agree an assessment plan with candidates;
- judge evidence against criteria to make assessment decisions;

- provide feedback and support to candidates on assessment decisions;
- contribute to the internal quality assurance process.

Candidates should have received any necessary induction and training they need in order to complete the unit *prior to planning for the assessment*. If this does not happen, candidates and assessors may find that the process becomes confused and unnecessarily prolonged. It is unfair to start the assessment planning process before candidates are ready to demonstrate competence and knowledge.

Assessors should check that candidates are registered with their awarding body prior to starting assessment. Submissions for certification of NVQs and mini-awards cannot be made within 10 weeks of registration.

A1.1: DEVELOP PLANS FOR ASSESSING COMPETENCE WITH CANDIDATES

(a) Develop and agree an assessment plan with candidates

The assessment process starts with planning between the assessor and the candidate. Each unit needs its own assessment plan. The plan needs to cover the whole unit. This process will be documented, and include arrangements for reviewing and updating the plan as circumstances change. The process needs to be agreed, so negotiation may need to take place. Dated signatures of both assessor and candidate are taken as confirmation of agreement.

A good starting point is getting the candidate to talk through what they do at present in relation to the unit in question. This should suggest the types of evidence that are most suitable for demonstrating competence, and the methods for assessment. The assessment plan documentation should allow all the details for the assessment for the whole unit to be noted.

The assessment plan should give a clear indication of *what* will be assessed, *how* it will be assessed and *when* it will be assessed. There will need to be reference to others, such as witnesses, workplace and independent assessors and the internal verifiers, who will all need to be involved. The candidate(s) will need to have an input into the plan (particularly in thinking through the other people who will be involved in the assessment), be able to ask any questions and be able to offer any appropriate suggestions or amendments. The assessment plan should indicate what competences or criteria are being assessed and clearly identify the appropriate methods that the assessor will use to make their decisions regarding the candidates' competence. It should indicate when and how feedback will be given, what records will be made of achievement, and how and when the plan will be reviewed. It should be clear to the candidates how they will know when they have achieved competence for the whole unit, and how this will be recorded.

(b) Check that all candidates understand the assessment process involved, the support available to them and the complaints and appeals procedure

Your candidates' understanding of the planning process can be checked through the asking of open questions, such as 'so how do you think. . .?', 'what will happen next. . .?'. Ask them to identify the support they think is available. Support might include their assessor, a learning centre, work colleagues, awarding body literature and Web sites. Make sure that candidates have a copy of the complaints and appeals process that will have been agreed by the external verifier with the centre. Question your candidates to check their understanding, and knowledge of how and when it might be used (though, of course, the fact that assessors will follow best practice after using this book and following all available advice should render this unlikely!). Keep notes of the discussion so you can each have a copy of them at the end of the session.

(c) Agree fair, safe, valid and reliable assessment methods

Assessors should plan to use at least four methods of assessment with candidates to assess their competence and underpinning knowledge. These methods can include assessing the prior experience of the candidate, questioning, professional discussion, workplace observation by a qualified assessor, the use of witness statements, simulations in an agreed limited range of contexts for some NVQs (but no simulation is allowed for A1, A2 or V1 candidates), projects and assignments. Chapter 2 gives additional information that should help you to meet these criteria.

(d) Identify appropriate and cost-effective opportunities for assessing performance

Direct observation of performance can take a considerable amount of time and be costly in terms of the assessor's time and the candidates' costs, but several elements of a unit or of several units could be covered in one well-planned observation visit. Opportunities for assessment of competence will generally occur during candidates' normal work time. You, the assessor, need to check with the candidates that time(s) and place(s) arranged for the assessment are as natural and efficient for all parties as possible. Candidates should be involved in identifying these opportunities and selecting those that will be the most convenient and offer the possibility of covering a number of elements.

The cost of assessment materials will also play a part in efficiency of assessment; it is cheaper to work with farmed salmon than cod these days! Assessor and candidate need to decide whether assessment of non-performance evidence and the professional discussion is likely to be more cost-effective if done at the candidate's workplace, close to his or her documentary evidence and possible witnesses, or at the primary assessor's premises. It is important to estimate in advance the time that each assessment is likely to take, and the breadth of criteria that will be assessed, so that neither party is disadvantaged by cost or by an unplanned lengthy or, just as bad, too short visit.

(e) Plan for using different types of evidence

See Chapter 3 for a fuller explanation. The use of as wide a variety of relevant types of evidence as possible will give your candidates the opportunity to show depth of understanding, the complexity of what they do, and a range of ways of working over time with their own vocational candidates.

(f) Identify how the past experiences and achievements of candidates will contribute to the assessment process

When candidates wish to use evidence from accreditation of prior learning (APL), an issue to consider is the recency of their evidence of competence. A candidate producing a computing qualification dating from the late 1970s will not be providing evidence of *current* competence in modern computer technology, whereas a qualification that is only one year old may well be acceptable. Currency of competence is obviously particularly important in areas where technology is in use; however, there may be other areas – eg the care sector – where a qualification obtained a number of years ago may still be judged appropriate and sufficient. You and the candidate need to check via the internal verifier for the NVQ in question to determine whether the awarding body has set time limits on past experience and achievements. Witnesses' statements and testimonials referring to past competence need to clearly identify the criteria the candidate has met. Original certificates for qualifications will need to be produced by the candidate. It could be that the professional discussion could be planned to allow the candidate to explain the evidence from prior assessments, experience or learning. Candidate and assessor need to discuss whether this evidence is likely to give proof of performance competence or of knowledge, and how it is likely to correlate with the required performance criteria and knowledge.

(g) Identify and agree any special arrangements needed to make sure the process is fair

Candidates for assessment should have received all necessary training and practice prior to their assessment. A candidate who normally worked on a night shift but was asked by his or her assessor to be assessed during the daytime would not have been given access to fair assessment. The candidate would be in an unfamiliar situation, and might experience poor concentration and disorientation owing to being on a different shift. Nor would the assessment give a reliable indication of how that person could perform in normal circumstances. Figure 3.3 (page 47) gives some examples of the difficulties that might be experienced by candidates.

(h) Identify how other people will contribute to assessments and what support they may need

The primary assessor will make the majority of assessments, but he or she may be assisted in this process by a number of others, such as:

- other workplace assessors with whom the assessor may need to co-ordinate;
- credible witnesses, who will need to write statements or talk to the primary assessor;
- an independent assessor, to whom the candidate will need to send agreed evidence;
- internal verifiers, who may request to sample the assessments.

In addition, the following will be or could be involved:

- line managers or supervisors, who may wish to be involved with feedback;
- technical staff to make sure the appropriate facilities are available;
- quality co-ordinators or managers, who may need reports;
- candidates' colleagues who may be affected;
- administration staff for processing registrations and certification requests;
- caretakers, car parking and security staff.

Many of these other people will not need support as such, but will be involved as part of the quality and administration process surrounding assessment.

(i) Identify how to protect confidentiality and agree arrangements to deal with sensitive issues

Candidates need to know what arrangements the assessor will make to keep their work safe. The demands of legislation will need to be followed. Both parties will need to comply with the Data Protection Act and the Mental Health Act regarding the disclosure of information about candidates, and decide how to assess necessary documentary evidence that cannot be removed from the workplace, while meeting the requirements of the Copyright Act. Candidate and assessor also need to clarify whether there are any sensitivities surrounding the assessment, such as difficulties with staff, premises or other organizations that need to be addressed prior to the assessment.

(j) Agree how you will handle any difficulties or disputes during the assessment

Discussion during this planning stage should reduce the likelihood of difficulties or disagreement. It is important that the assessor is clear about what is or is not negotiable, and candidates should be made aware of this. For example, if the awarding body requires a written test, candidates must complete this even though they may be unwilling. The option here is basically 'Do it, because if you don't, you can't get the qualification.' However, you would obviously take into account whether a candidate is objecting because he or she needs encouragement or more guidance in order to provide this sort of evidence.

It may be that you cannot resolve the difficulties yourself. You may suggest another assessor to the candidate or suggest that he or she talks to the internal verifier. You may feel that it would help if the candidate talked to other candidates who have been through the process.

If assessments have to be cancelled by either party, there need to be clear lines of communication, and guidelines to minimize disruption and to facilitate the earliest possible reassessment opportunity.

The most likely problem will be that the candidate disagrees with the assessor's judgement, or that the assessor and candidate cannot find common times to carry out assessments. Both parties need to be clear about the options available – for example, whether the use of another assessor is possible. The complaints and appeals procedure is there as a last resort.

(k) Agree when assessment will take place with candidates and the other people involved

It is most helpful to everyone involved for dates and times to be set early for the different assessment activities planned, even though some may need to be rescheduled, eg because of bad weather or illness. Negotiating dates with the candidate gives targets for achievement, and should be a motivating experience. Any changes will need to be noted on the assessment plan. If you or your candidate find it difficult to set dates during your planning session, it may be worth considering whether the candidate is at the right stage to begin the assessment process. The candidate may need a longer period of training, or may need to involve his or her workplace more fully in the process before proceeding. Failure to set dates usually results in an unsatisfactorily long period before candidates complete their award.

(l) Agree arrangements with candidates for reviewing their progress against the assessment plan

Agreeing arrangements for reviewing progress is best done following feedback sessions from each formative assessment. It could be done face to face, by telephone or via e-mail contact.

(m) Review and update assessment plans to take account of what the candidates have achieved

The review will result in the assessment plan being physically updated, with new dates and actions. If the candidate is not physically present at the review, but has verbally agreed, or responded to e-mail, the assessor will need to send an updated copy of the assessment plan to the candidate as soon as possible. Reviews should always be documented in some way and any revision of assessment plans recorded on them, and signed and dated by both parties at the time, as evidence of agreement.

A1.2: JUDGE EVIDENCE AGAINST CRITERIA TO MAKE ASSESSMENT DECISIONS

(a) Use the agreed assessment methods to assess competence in appropriate situations

The A1.1 plan will state the assessment methods that the assessor and candidate have agreed will be used unless amendments are negotiated and agreed between the candidate and the assessor. To achieve A1, the assessor candidate will need to use a minimum of four appropriate assessment methods across three assessment plans. Most assessment methods are easily linked to particular situations – for instance, evidence of performance is best assessed through observation or witness testimony, and evidence of knowledge and understanding through questioning, testing or professional discussion.

(b) Use the past experiences and achievements of candidates as part of the assessment of their current competence

Planning will have helped candidates to identify what evidence from their past achievements and experiences is relevant to the assessment of their competence. It is wasteful for candidates to repeat activities or qualifications that they have assimilated into their everyday practice. Their skills and knowledge should become apparent as the foundation of their current practice. If in doubt, the most straightforward way of checking current achievement is to ask candidates to carry out the relevant process or activity. For instance, assessors could ask to see candidates carry out a number of different functions using a modern computer, or ask them to explain how their background affects their current practice. Letters of validation or witness testimonies carefully linked to the standards might be sufficient to confirm some of the competences claimed, though assessors should always check the authenticity of witnesses.

(c) Ensure that the evidence comes from the candidate's own work

Where assessment is based on documentary evidence or made products, you will need to ask questions so that you can be assured that the candidate concerned has been the originator of the evidence. Few candidates deliberately cheat. However, misunderstandings can result in candidates including written documents produced by their organizations or their trainers rather than themselves.

Professional discussion allows the assessor the opportunity to check a range of queries they might have after assessing the different strands of evidence. The assessor, having made a judgement and given feedback, can prepare the candidate for the discussion by identifying the areas where they feel more explanation or evidence is needed. The assessor-candidate can then share their ideas, knowledge, understanding and practice with the assessor, through discussion, which would ideally be held at the candidates' workplace, and led by the candidate. The discussion could include backing up what is said by reference to documents, products or other persons in the workplace.

(d) Make safe, fair, valid and reliable decisions about the competence of candidates only on the agreed standard

Safety, fairness, validity and reliability are explored in Chapter 3. Once the assessor is presented with evidence – eg an observation report, a witness statement, a set of written answers or evidence of prior achievement – this must be assessed using the agreed methods against the standards. Studies have shown that, in general, the degree of error made by NVQ assessors is about the same as that made by assessors of public written exams, and that, overall, assessors' judgements are sound.

Noting down why, as an assessor, you have decided that certain evidence meets or does not meet the standards is good practice, and should form part of the written feedback to candidates. It should help with minimizing the risk of subjectivity and/or bias. It is good practice to date each assessment you make and to record the results immediately. In order to be fair and reliable, you must ensure that the knowledge you want the candidate to demonstrate is closely tied in to what is identified in the element and does not wander into the realms of 'what you think the candidate should know'. For example, NVQ retailing has an element on unpacking stock, and one knowledge requirement relates to the candidate's responsibilities under the Health and Safety at Work Act. The assessor needs to be clear that, in this instance, he or she is only assessing the candidate's knowledge of health and safety in relation to unpacking goods, including lifting, carrying and the correct use of equipment.

(e) Collect evidence from the other people involved in the assessment process

Collecting evidence from other people about your candidates should be done in the most effective and cost-efficient ways, whether by telephone, e-mail, written documents, face-to-face meetings or via your candidate. Keep records of how you obtained the evidence, and how you checked the authenticity of witnesses. Your internal verifier should check how assessors approach authentication and validating of witness statements.

(f) Apply any agreed special arrangements to make sure the assessment is fair

Language, ethnicity and gender issues have been studied as areas where fairness might be compromised. Translators or signers may need to be used for some candidates. Examples and situations that are not dependent on being fully familiar with British culture should be used where possible, as long as the integrity of the assessment is not compromised. Assessors should be careful that their judgements are not influenced when assessing women in traditionally male roles and vice versa.

(g) Base all your decisions on all the relevant evidence of candidates' performance and knowledge

It is only by studying the totality of candidates' evidence that the assessor is in a position to decide on whether candidates have met the standards, so it is necessary to base your decisions on *all* the relevant evidence. Take this from as many places as possible. (See Table 6.1)

When we look at someone carrying out an activity, we can often see that the individual knows how to do something under a particular set of circumstances. This may be sufficient for the knowledge requirements you are assessing. For example, in NVQ level 2 in Retailing, the element involving recognition of hazardous goods and substances has a knowledge requirement that the candidate should know the location and use of protective clothing and equipment. When assessing, you might observe the candidate go to a storeroom or locker and put on some appropriate protective clothing. It would then be quite reasonable to infer that the candidate had filled that particular knowledge requirement related to the element.

We can often infer a good deal about what someone knows by what they do or what they produce. For example, if we observe someone involved in child care instructing small children to wash their hands before eating, we can infer that the child care assistant knows at least one basic rule of hygiene. Similarly, if we are shown a completed press article produced by a journalist, we can infer that the journalist knows how to structure information and spell words correctly. However, we must be very careful in inferring how *much* someone knows from what we see him or her do. In the first example given, the child care assistant could just be copying what he has seen others do, without any knowledge of the reason why he is doing it. In this case he probably has no concept of the 'idea' of hygiene and hence would not be able to transfer this rule across to another situation. In the case of the journalist, we may be satisfied that she has produced the article herself, but has she had her spelling and grammar checked by others or used a computer spell or grammar check? Has she used a standard format to structure her article? In both examples, the key to assessing whether someone really knows something needs to be taken from the level of qualification. At lower levels, the definition of knowledge could just involve 'has information about', and the understanding required could be very limited. At higher levels, the definition of knowledge will probably include a deeper understanding of the knowledge aspects related to the element, plus a broader ability to transfer and make connections between ideas and practice.

There are obviously difficulties in inferring knowledge from performance, particularly at higher levels. A notable exception to this is where the product evidence itself contains evidence of knowledge and understanding, such as a formal in-depth report on organizational training needs produced by a candidate involved in human resource development and presented as evidence for an NVQ in Learning and Development.

You, as the assessor, need to be fully familiar with the standards your candidates must achieve, and be confident that your decision is supported by their evidence. If you have any doubt, ask your internal verifier for advice.

(h) Explain and resolve any inconsistencies in the evidence

As you are making a judgement of someone's competence based on a range of evidence, there may be occasions where the level of competence suggested by one piece of evidence is not supported by other evidence. For example, you may have a written testimonial from a previous employer stating that the candidate always followed health and safety procedures, but one observational assessor's report states that there were instances when this had not happened. In this case, you would give the candidate feedback that he or she had not met this requirement consistently and that during the next observation, this competence would need to be satisfactorily demonstrated. In order to be sure, you would probably question the candidate closely about his or her understanding of health and safety procedures and look for additional third-party evidence as well, eg from the candidate's supervisor at work.

Another example is of an NVQ Business Administration candidate, assessed by a number of observational assessors, who appears to be having little difficulty in achieving elements related to filing, but a great deal of difficulty with elements related to stock-keeping. This might raise an issue regarding the candidate's numeracy skills. To check these, you might see how she is doing on her Key Skill 'Application of Number'. If her numerical ability is adequate, has she understood her stock-keeping training? If she does not have any problems with her assessors, and no particular dislike of this area of work, you might look more closely at the level of consistency among assessors. Are some expecting more than the standards require? Clarification will probably come by talking to the candidate and to other assessors, and by asking for advice from the internal verifier.

The most worrying form of inconsistency is that where you suspect cheating, plagiarism or some other form of malpractice. If after checking the evidence with the candidate you still have doubts, contact the internal verifier or the awarding body as soon as possible for advice.

(i) Make a record of the outcomes of assessments by using the agreed recording system

As your candidates' primary assessor, you are likely to make several formative assessments as well as a summative judgement on the different types of agreed evidence for a whole unit. You will use at least four assessment methods in making this overall judgement. Once you are sure of your decision, enter your findings into the system – paper or IT based – used by your centre. There should be a tracking sheet where you record the criteria that the candidate has achieved, with the dates of assessments, and space to record who made the assessment decisions. If a candidate has successfully met the criteria for a complete unit, this will need entering on the record of achievement. You should make written notes to support your decisions that will remind you of the types of evidence you have reviewed, the methods used for assessment and why the evidence met or did not meet criteria. You may want to record what was particularly good or particularly weak about the evidence. This record will provide the basis of feedback to your candidate, and will also assist external and internal verifiers in their auditing processes.

(j) Speak to the appropriate person if you and the candidate cannot agree on the assessment of their performance

Disagreements are most likely to come about because you think the candidate is not yet competent, and the candidate thinks that his or her evidence is proof of competence. Your records should show you and the candidate the basis for your decision. It could be that you have misinterpreted some evidence given to you, in which case you can check that out, but the better course of action would be to involve your internal verifier, who can review your decision and verify its accuracy (or otherwise).

A1.3: PROVIDE FEEDBACK AND SUPPORT TO CANDIDATES ON ASSESSMENT DECISIONS

(a) Give candidates feedback at an appropriate time and place

It is not enough just to tell a candidate that he or she has been successful or not. Your role is also to let the candidate know why you have made that decision. This is why the assessor should always set aside a proper time for discussion with the candidate so that both have time to talk over the result, and the assessor is sure that the candidate fully understands the reasons for the assessment decision.

For candidates who have not met the demands of the unit, it is particularly important that they are given specific indications of what they need to do, or how they need to improve, in a constructive way that will enable them to move forward to successful assessment. The reasons supporting the assessment decision should be noted in writing in the assessment feedback related to the relevant units. Ideally, this feedback will be given as soon after the assessment as possible, in a place where neither of you is likely to be disturbed. Arrangements for feedback should have been detailed on the assessment plan.

(b) Give candidates feedback in a constructive and encouraging way that meets their needs and is appropriate to their level of confidence

All candidates need to know how well they did and why, and to know how they might improve. Candidates will have been judged on the standards – that is, they have met or not met the standard. However, they can be told what was particularly good about their performance, or where their performance though competent could benefit from continued attention. Some candidates will have a good deal of confidence and competence. For other candidates, the feedback process is essential to motivate and move them forward. In all cases, the feedback should be seen as development and not just as an end in itself. Note down the key points of oral feedback for the candidate. It is often forgotten, as relief or anxiety can block the messages the assessor is giving. The relationship you established with the candidate at the planning stage will be crucial in ensuring that feedback is received positively and is useful to the candidate. Encourage discussion of the assessment, and try to get the candidate to explain whether any changes to process might help future assessment. In addition, your IV will need to know *how* and *what* you are feeding back to your candidate as he or she samples your decisions.

(c) Clearly explain your assessment decisions on whether candidates' evidence of competence is good enough

You need to be able to justify your decisions objectively, and you can do this only by referring to the range of evidence you have assessed, and showing the candidate how you matched this to the performance criteria. The notes you took as you reviewed the evidence should help you here. You should be able, as a vocationally competent assessor, to reassure the candidate that you are assessing against industry standards, and not your personal view of 'acceptable' work.

You may not have been prepared to judge the candidate competent on the evidence available. This could occur when the candidate has not provided evidence of sufficient quality. For example, the candidate has brought you a witness testimony written by a line manager, but it is so general that it does not back up the candidate's claim against specific elements. You might have to ask the candidate to get another, more specific statement, or you might decide that you will arrange to observe him or her at work instead.

Another situation could be that a candidate has enough evidence against the performance criteria, but has not shown that he or she meets the range or scope of the unit. In this case, you will discuss in feedback what else the candidate needs to do.

Yet another example could be where a candidate has written answers to pre-set knowledge questions, but they are minimal in content. In this case, you might agree with the candidate that professional discussion will give him or her the opportunity to show greater depth and breadth of knowledge and understanding.

Whatever the problem is, candidates should be left with a clear idea of what they need to do, and the assessment plan should be updated accordingly. The written records will be used by the internal verifier in checking the accuracy of your assessments and your monitoring of candidate's progress.

(d) Give candidates advice when they cannot prove their competence and on how they can develop the necessary skills or provide more evidence

Candidates can be held up from proving their competence if their own NVQ candidates leave, or are finding difficulty in completing their own units. Another problematic area is where a candidate is not linked into the centre's internal verification procedures in a satisfactory way. These circumstances can delay in particular the assessment opportunities for A1 and V1 candidates.

Assessors may be able to encourage the candidate to liaise more effectively with key centre staff (line mangers, internal verifiers) to ensure that suitable candidates are available and that internal procedures support the candidate's achievement. It is clear that thorough initial planning and liaison between assessor and centre can help to prevent these problems developing in the first place. Training, either one to one or group, may be available via the centre, the awarding body or the NTO responsible, and the assessor can help the candidate to access this. Assessors can also ensure that they have access to relevant texts and Web sites to help develop general subject knowledge and specific knowledge in assessment and verification (see the end of the book for some useful references and Web sites).

(e) Encourage candidates to get advice on your assessment decisions

The relationship you have built should enable candidates to ask why or how you or others involved in their assessment arrived at their decisions, and to challenge those decisions if they are unclear or unhappy about them.

(f) Identify and agree the next steps in the assessment process and how candidates will achieve these

Go back to the assessment plan and check whether it needs amending, or simply updating. If a complete unit has been signed off, a completely new plan for the next unit needs to be agreed.

(g) Follow the agreed complaints and appeals procedures if candidates disagree with your assessment decisions

You and the candidate will have gone through this procedure in your assessment planning session, and the candidate should have access to the written procedure. Hopefully, neither of you will need to implement it. If you do start to follow the procedure, keep careful notes of what you have done and said. You should of course have documentary evidence of all your planning, assessment decisions and feedback.

A1.4: CONTRIBUTE TO THE INTERNAL QUALITY ASSURANCE PROCESS

(a) Ensure your assessment records are accurate and up to date, and can be followed by an auditor

You will have a number of documents to complete during the assessment process. These may be produced by your organization, or they may be documents produced by the awarding body. For each unit a candidate works through, you should have completed as a minimum:

- one assessment plan, reviewed and dated, with evidence of negotiation;
- a tracking document logging the various dates of achievement of performance criteria/range/scope/ knowledge and understanding, as detailed in the relevant standards;
- feedback sheets dated and signed;
- records of achievement dated and signed.

The best way of ensuring accuracy is to enter information as it is negotiated or fed back to the candidate, and for both of you to sign and date documents there and then to confirm agreement and accuracy. These dates and signatures provide an audit trail that an auditor (ie an internal verifier or external verifier) can use to track any aspect of the assessment process against the appropriate standards.

The importance of meticulous record keeping cannot be overestimated in the assessment process. However, in order for the audit trail to work, the system needs to be simple, legible and credible. If mistakes are made in the recording, they should be altered clearly, and signed to indicate that the error has been corrected by the assessor and not altered without authority, much as you would initial a correction on a cheque. Correction fluid should not be used. You need to pass on records promptly to ensure that you avoid hoarding documents on your shelf, desk or filing cabinet, which would prevent other assessors, verifiers or any centralized recording system from inputting the information on candidates' achievements, and therefore possibly preventing candidates' access to the qualification.

(b) Contribute to standardization arrangements so that your assessment decisions are in line with others'

An internal verifier should manage you in your organization. He or she should be regularly sampling all types of assessment decisions and should also hold standardization sessions where you will have the opportunity to check that you are making the same decisions on evidence as would other assessors. Often these meetings use anonymous photocopied unit evidence from real candidates, which is judged independently by each member of the assessment team. The results of the assessments are then compared and discussed, allowing differences of interpretation to be resolved.

(c) Give accurate and timely information on assessments

Your organization is likely to have at least three audit points in a year. Internal verifiers will need to know how you are progressing with your workload on a regular basis, and will request quantitative and qualitative data from assessors.

(d) Contribute to the agreed quality assurance process

There will be centre verification procedures for both internal and external verification. Many organizations have their own system of recording, feedback, assessment decisions and candidate progress. Relevant details are then transferred across to meet external awarding body requirements. Discussions are usually held with external verifiers to ensure that there is no unnecessary duplication of information. All assessors should be included within the process. Contributions to the process could include attending meetings, providing qualitative and quantitative data (see Figure 6.1 which shows the consequences of insufficient data regarding dates), being observed, discussing decisions and completing documentation accurately and promptly. Assessors may be requested to submit assessment decisions for sampling or for standardization purposes at any point during candidates' progress.

Whatever the quality assurance process used for verification by a centre, it should have been agreed with the relevant awarding body for each qualification offered.

6

Guide to Unit A2: Assess Candidates' Performance through Observation

Unit A2 has four elements:

- A2.1: Agree and review plans for assessing candidates' performance.
- A2.2: Assess candidates' performance against the agreed standards.
- A2.3: Assess candidates' knowledge against the agreed standards.
- A2.4: Make an assessment decision and provide feedback.

This award is for those assessors who carry out important but more restricted assessment than A1 assessors. They observe candidates carrying out competence-based tasks in the workplace, and assess candidates' competence against performance criteria and the related knowledge. They cannot act as independent assessors for A1 candidates.

A2.1: AGREE AND REVIEW PLANS FOR ASSESSING CANDIDATES' PERFORMANCE

Remembering what is said about the different stages in the assessment process in Chapter 3, you will recognize A2.1 as the 'planning stage' where you reach agreement with your vocational candidate about *what* will be assessed, how the assessment will be carried out and *when* it will take place. You will be ensuring that there is no confusion about the suitability of the evidence and that all the arrangements for the assessment have been organized and agreed.

(a) Identify the best situations when you can assess performance

The assessor needs to help candidates relate what they are doing as part of their normal work to the units and elements to be assessed so that together they *both* can identify the possible opportunities for assessment. The assessments should be done as part of a normal working shift, when the candidate is naturally carrying out performance tasks. Observations should be planned to cover as many elements and performance criteria as possible and the candidate needs to estimate the time likely to be taken. Issues to be considered will be the impact of observations on normal working, holidays and potential sickness, the preparation required, the commitments of the assessor, and the times when the candidate is most likely to be able to receive face-to-face feedback directly following the assessment.

(b) Use evidence that takes place in the workplace and ask relevant questions

Your assessment should be based on what the candidate is doing as a natural part of his or her work and on your observation of 'natural' performance. The starting point for discussion with the candidate is what evidence could be used to prove competence – that is, begin with what is already there in what the candidate is actually doing, rather than what needs more work to produce or design. Assessors need to check, through the use of open questions, any aspect of the planned observation that is unclear to them, so that risk of an ineffective visit is minimized.

(c) Choose opportunities for assessment that disrupt normal work as little as possible

Involving candidates' supervisors in the planning process should enable candidates to plan work-based assessment opportunities into their normal work routines with as little disruption as possible. Having an assessor around is likely to alter the dynamics of situations, and increase the nerves of both the candidate (and *their* candidates, if the NVQ is process rather than product based). Of course, in some situations candidates will be used to being observed on a regular basis. For example, in a motor vehicle workshop, supervisory staff will be moving around all the time checking on work being done. Similarly, in an open-learning workshop, candidates will be used to staff circulating and being available for consultation. In situations such as these, candidates are less likely to be disturbed than in a situation where candidates are not used to being observed; for example, a candidate being assessed as a trainer may never have had an observer with him or her in the training situation.

The assessments should be organized so that candidates demonstrating their competence do not experience unnecessary disruption to their work routine. Assessors need to be conscious of the work environment and ensure that feedback and questioning following assessment keep within planned timescales.

(d) Choose opportunities for assessment that provide access to a valid, safe, reliable and fair assessment

See Chapter 3 for a fuller explanation of these terms. Safety must be considered in both the physical sense and the sense of being sure that the decision is sound. The only time an assessor should interfere in an assessment is if there is potential or actual harm to those involved. The assessor should have enough evidence to be sure that the candidate can perform competently and consistently over time.

(e) Explain the options open to the candidates clearly and constructively if somebody disagrees with the assessment plan

The candidates will need the opportunity to discuss the proposed assessment plan with workplace colleagues and their own candidates, but before they do this, both of you need to clarify what is or is not negotiable in terms of the assessment. Rearrangement of time or place, choice of different units for candidates (and even of different candidates), materials to be used, types of evidence and witnesses are all negotiable. Non-negotiable for A2 is the agreed common evidence (detailed with all sets of the standards) which details the number of plans, reviews, records and statements to be provided by the assessor-candiate.

(f) Discuss and agree the proposed assessment plan with the candidates and other people who may be affected

Once the candidate understands what is and is not negotiable, the plan needs to be shared with everyone who may be affected. The assessment plan should give a clear indication of *what* will be assessed, *how* it will be assessed and *when* it will be assessed. Only after this can the plan be finally agreed. Signing and dating by both parties is the convention used to denote agreement. It is important that this signing and dating is done as soon as the plan has been agreed. The other people who could be affected by the planned assessment will vary according to the work situation, but they might include:

- supervisors in the workplace who might need to adjust staffing rotas;
- witnesses who may be required to provide written statements;
- other tutors or trainers who need to co-ordinate their assessments with yours;
- technical staff, to make sure that the appropriate facilities were made available;
- the internal verifier, who will need to include you as an assessor and your assessments in their sampling plan;
- candidates' colleagues who might be affected by the presence of an assessor.

(g) Review and update plans at agreed times to take account of candidates' progress

One of the problems with working on assessments with candidates who are on a programme dependent on the progress and co-operation of others, possibly on different sites from the primary assessor, is the danger that they will feel isolated or let other work take priority. Assessors need to be aware of this and develop a system for keeping in contact, regularly reviewing progress. The way you decide to do this will depend largely on the experience of the candidate and the amount of support and motivation he or she needs from you.

As the candidate achieves targets, and as circumstances change, the plan will need amending and updating. It is crucial that the first workplace assessments take place as soon after the completion of the assessment plan as possible. This will enable the candidate to use feedback constructively and maintain motivation. The timescale for achievement needs to be realistic and the assessor needs to help the candidate maintain progress via regular planned reviews and updates.

A2.2: ASSESS CANDIDATES' PERFORMANCE AGAINST THE AGREED STANDARDS

Having dealt with the planning for assessment, assessor and candidate can move on to the actual process of assessing performance evidence.

(a) Explain to candidates how the assessment of their work will take account of their needs

Different candidates will need different levels of support, depending on factors such as their maturity, their experience at performing the required tasks and their understanding of what they have learnt regarding the associated knowledge. Some candidates will have specific needs that should have been identified during the induction and assessment planning phases. Refer to Figure 3.3 (page 47) concerning barriers to access to be reminded of the range of special assessment needs.

All candidates will need to be reassured that the assessor will make some allowance for initial nerves. Assessors will start building relationships with candidates during the assessment planning process that hopefully will lead to as relaxed an observation as possible.

(b) Watch candidates in a safe environment

The assessment environment must meet the requirements of the Health and Safety at Work Act. All participants in the assessment have a responsibility for reporting any unsafe environment, equipment or practices. The assessor must conform to any additional health and safety rules determined by the workplace, such as the wearing of protective clothing. The only time you, as assessor, should interfere with an assessment you are observing is if you, the candidate or his or her own candidates appear to be at risk.

(c) Only use the agreed criteria when assessing the evidence

You must not deviate from the agreed criteria when making your judgements. Even if you are convinced that receptionists should smile at their clients, but this is not included in the standard, then it is invalid and unfair to use it as a criterion for assessment. Make notes of any performance that appears to be *beyond* the requirements of the standards (ie smiling, in the case of the receptionists). This will be good for positive developmental feedback, and may form good evidence for the candidate for another unit, or even evidence against a future assessment at a higher level.

(d) Assess evidence fairly against the agreed criteria

Fairness in assessment is covered in Chapter 3. Assessors need to be sure that they are judging all candidates according to their performance against the identified criteria, and not against what the assessor *thinks* they can do, or thinks they *should* do. It is easy to want to give candidates 'the benefit of the doubt', but the candidates need to show they are competent at performing all the standards in their everyday work.

Just as unfair would be refusing to accept that a candidate is competent because of the lack of a skill that may not be required for the competence being assessed. Legibility of handwriting and the ability to speak fluently might be crucial to the achievement of competences for a candidate in administration, but might not be part of the standards for an IT candidate. Assessors need to be very familiar with the standards that are being used for the assessment.

(e) Identify and assess any other evidence that is relevant to the standards

The assessor should now have an idea of whether candidates have 'gaps' in their competence or knowledge. At this stage of the assessment process, the assessor will need to determine with the candidates how these gaps will be closed. A suitable method at this stage will be professional discussion, which, if planned well and held at the candidates' workplace, should enable candidates to explain, show or reinforce by activity any aspects of their performance or knowledge and understanding that are currently unclear to the assessor.

(f) Check that the evidence has come from each candidate's own work

Because performance evidence is generally generated through the observation of natural performance, the observational assessor should see candidates do the work and question them personally to establish competence or achievement across the range. However, there will be some situations where this is less clear-cut. Safeguards will have to be in place to ensure that evidence from prior experience or learning is the candidates' own. For example, if a candidate in catering showed you a cake he had prepared, you might ask him to describe how he had made it, what ingredients he used, and the temperature he used while cooking it. In fact, you should ask as many questions as you needed to ask to feel sure that he knew what he was talking about. You still might not be satisfied, so you might ask to talk to his supervisor, who could confirm that the candidate had made the cake, or, if that was not possible, to review a witness statement which stated that the cake was the normal standard of work of the candidate.

Assessors should check out any evidence, such as product evidence or APL, that has not been assessed by an accredited assessor.

(g) Watch candidates without interfering with their work

There is sometimes a temptation when observing, to 'fit in' with the candidates, and thus skew the dynamics of the relationship between the candidate and their own vocational candidates or work pattern. In order to assess accurately against the elements and performance criteria agreed in the assessment plan, assessors may need to be very close to the candidate for particular operations, perhaps to see what the candidate is doing or to hear what he or she is saying to a client. In cases like this, you may well be noticeable, but not interfering. Assessors will obviously try their best to distract the candidate and their clients as little as possible. This will require discussion with the candidate and client, who can advise where the assessor should position him- or herself. What assessors must *not* do is contribute to the assessment in any way by offering information or advice, by asking questions or by showing how to perform tasks.

(h) Speak to the appropriate person if you or a candidate has any difficulties

Difficulties can occur at all stages of the process, due to, for example, late arrivals, faulty equipment, client behaviour, or the acoustics of the observation environment. If the assessment needs to be repeated for any reason, then the same people who needed informing the first time will need to be informed again. If any additional training or workplace adjustments need to be made, or the assessments need to be rearranged because of difficulties on either side, then again the relevant people will need to be informed.

(i) Give candidates feedback after you have watched them in the workplace

Candidates desperately need to know what they have achieved and how well they have done. They also need to know how to improve further (even if all performance criteria have been met). Just to tell candidates whether they are competent or not is not enough. Your role is also to let them know why you have made that decision. This is why the assessor should always set aside a proper time for discussion with the candidate so that both have time to talk over the result and the assessor is sure that the candidate fully understands the reasons for the assessment decision. Obviously, for candidates who have not yet achieved competence, it is particularly important that they are given specific indications of where they need to improve, in a constructive way that will motivate them for the next time they are assessed. See Figure 3.5 on page 56 for more information on this. Feedback is best given orally, as soon after the observation as possible. It should be backed up with written notes, with a copy for the candidate. If face-to-face feedback is not possible following the observation, written notes can be left with the candidate to read through, and a date and time fixed as soon as possible to go through the notes.

A2.3: ASSESS CANDIDATES' KNOWLEDGE AGAINST THE AGREED STANDARDS

(a) Identify which areas of candidates' knowledge have been covered by watching them in the workplace

All NVQ qualifications have defined knowledge that needs to be assessed as part of the candidates' competence. In some NVQs this knowledge is tightly defined, with model answers being provided for assessors. In others, there is more room for broader interpretation by assessors as to what the required minimum knowledge might be, particularly in the higher levels of qualifications.

When we look at someone carrying out an activity, we can usually tell that the individual knows how to do something under a particular set of circumstances. This may be sufficient for the knowledge requirements you are assessing. For example, in NVQ level 2 in Retailing, the element involving recognition of hazardous goods and substances has a knowledge requirement that the candidate should know the location and use of protective clothing and equipment. When assessing, you might observe the candidate go to a storeroom or locker and put on some protective clothing. It would then be quite reasonable to infer that the candidate had filled that particular knowledge requirement related to the element.

There are obviously difficulties in inferring knowledge from performance, particularly at higher levels. A notable exception to this is where the product evidence itself contains evidence of knowledge and understanding, such as a formal in-depth report on organizational training needs produced by a candidate involved in human resource development and presented as evidence for an NVQ in Learning and Development. Assessors need to be familiar with what their candidates need to know and be clear about whether this can really be inferred through observation, or whether additional activities will need to be used to collect the evidence required.

Assessors will need to check off the knowledge evidence that has been assessed, and note down candidates' responses if these are not in written form. Knowledge that has not been covered can be planned into professional discussion.

(b) Collect evidence of knowledge that has not been covered by watching the candidates in the workplace

Assessors will have anticipated in the planning phase what knowledge is likely to be evidenced through observation of performance. Estimates may need to be revised following observation, and further evidence sought. This may be just a matter of planning some additional topics into the professional discussion, or you may need to ask candidates to supply additional direct or indirect evidence.

(c) Use valid methods to assess candidates' knowledge

Knowledge has traditionally been assessed through tests and examinations. Assessing knowledge underpinning work-based performance is unlikely to involve either of these methods. Some inference of knowledge will be made by the assessor, but this needs to be backed up with questioning and professional discussion. Witness statements or judgements made by other assessors will help to give a rounded picture of the knowledge the candidate is demonstrating.

It is important to ensure that the assessment is on the knowledge, rather than factors connected with the evidence, such as communication skills. This is not, of course, to deny that communication skills are vitally important. It may be true that the candidate needs to address these, but unless they are clearly stated as being a prerequisite at a particular level, or are built into the standard in some way, they should not affect the knowledge judgement. Remembering the importance of removing barriers to access to assessment, candidates' particular needs should be taken into account – for example, whether it would be fairer to test them in writing or orally. Someone who had worked for many years at a machine on a factory floor might not have had to do much writing. To test that person's knowledge by setting him or her a written test could be unfair (unless of course it was a requirement of the awarding body) and might not produce a reliable indication of what the person really knows.

Table 6.1 Methods of knowledge assessment

Knowledge evidence gathered through:	Assessor needs to:
Observation of performance	Infer what candidate must know because of the quality of the performance
Questioning	Determine the minimum level and breadth of acceptability for answers
Professional discussion	Pre-plan discussion topics where clarification is needed. Encourage candidate to talk at ease about their role so they can show broad occupational competence. Ask probing questions where appropriate
Witness statements	Check authenticity and recency. Check status of witness – what qualifies him or her to make a judgement? Match statement to criteria
Qualifications	Check authenticity and recency; may need to look at whether updating is needed to bring candidate up to current occupational competence
Personal statements and explanations	Check for coverage of scope and knowledge
Assignments and projects	Assessment mark scheme needs clarifying and explaining to candidate prior to the start of candidate's work
Simulation	Check the areas allowed by the NTO and the awarding body guidance prior to accepting

Apart from this, you also need to consider the time and cost involved with different methods. Finding out what someone knows through professional discussion may be more time-consuming for the assessor than getting a group of candidates together for a written multiple-choice test. However, it is likely to be quicker and more rewarding for the candidate or organization, and, if planned to occur directly after observation, may take less time than anticipated. To check you are using these methods correctly, as usual talk with your internal verifier and be familiar with the awarding body guidelines. Table 6.1 above gives a wide range of methods of assessing knowledge. A2 assessors are likely (and expected) to use the first 3 methods in the table.

(d) Ask clear questions that do not 'lead' candidates

If oral or written questioning is to be used, each question should be specific, easy to understand and not phrased in such a way that an answer is suggested or a bias on the part of the assessor is indicated. For example, a question such as 'Don't you think you should have cleared the work area before you began the next job?' is hardly a question at all, but an indication that the assessor thinks that the candidate has done something wrong. You will find more examples of different types of questions in Chapter 4.

(e) Speak to the appropriate person if you or a candidate has any difficulties

See A2.2h (page 103).

(f) Give candidates feedback after you have asked them questions

Your preliminary questions will allow you to check out any areas of confusion, and clarify why the candidate chose to perform his or her tasks in particular ways. Feedback should always be constructive, especially if candidates have not met the criteria, and should be accompanied by written notes of the points for candidates, even if you give feedback orally. See Chapter 3 for advice on giving feedback.

A2.4: MAKE AN ASSESSMENT DECISION AND PROVIDE FEEDBACK

At this stage the assessor will have a good idea as to the candidate's overall competence, based not only on his or her own observations, but also from endorsements by other assessors, and the internal verifier's statement showing how the assessor has contributed to internal quality assurance procedures.

(a) Base your decision on all the relevant evidence

The evidence must include that from all others involved in the assessment process. You will have observed the candidate yourself, received feedback from and the judgements from other assessors, including the independent assessor, and have the internal verifier's statement. You will have the results of your professional discussion, and any additional work the candidate has done to provide sufficient evidence of knowledge. You make a positive decision about a candidate only when you have enough information to convince you that the candidate is able currently to meet all the criteria in the national standards.

(b) Give candidates clear and constructive feedback that meets their needs, after you have given them your assessment

The summative assessment needs to summarize the full extent of what has been achieved, and to detail what the candidate needs to do next. All records used in making the decision need to be available for both the candidate and the internal verifier.

You may have decided to confirm competence cumulatively, as the assessment progressed. As soon as the candidates have received the final assessment of 'competent' or 'not competent', they need feedback. Candidates who are not yet competent will need advice on what to do before they re-present themselves for final assessment. Those who are competent will need to know what they did particularly well; how they can continue to 'put the icing on the cake', and what to do next.

(c) Encourage candidates to ask for advice on your assessment decision

Face-to-face feedback will help candidates to reflect on your decision and to raise questions. You will have all your records to show the candidates, and this should help them to understand the decision, and what they need to do next.

When you have given feedback to a candidate, are you sure that he or she understands it? Are you sure that the candidate knows what to do with it? You may need to consider how you ensure that candidates have a proper opportunity to discuss the assessments with you, both in circumstances where they receive oral feedback face to face and where they receive written feedback. What means do you use in these situations to encourage them to discuss the assessment with you? How far are they aware of the feedback process and the active part they should play in order to get the most out of what they are told? All these are vital questions. The answers are not straightforward, but are bound up in the relationship that you manage to establish with the candidate.

(d) Make an accurate record of your assessment decisions

You need to check that all the details are entered on to the correct documentation, and that you have signed and dated the assessment. Using the convention dd/mm/yy for dates will be useful where any records for electronic data entering have to be made, and will give much more accuracy as to the speed of a candidate's progress. Labelling the start of an assessment process merely as June 04 and its completion merely as August 04 gives an uncertainty of two months regarding the time taken to achieve it (Figure 6.1).

01.06.03	01.06.03	30.06.03
31.08.03	01.08.03	01.08.03
3 months	2 months	1 month

Figure 6.1 Completion times possible when names of months only are given

(e) Pass on records that are accurate and easy to read to the next stage of the process

The importance of meticulous record keeping cannot be overestimated in the assessment process. In order for the records to be useful, all those entitled to see them, including verifiers, other assessors, appropriate administrative personnel and the candidates themselves, should be able to access and make sense of them. Handwritten records must be legible. Any mistakes made in the recording should be altered clearly and signed to indicate the error has been corrected by the assessor and not altered without authority. Results should be entered into records at the time the judgement is being made. Paper records might need to be transferred to electronic recording systems; this should be done as soon as possible, and the original paper record kept until at least after the next audit and the candidate has received his or her certificate. Many organizations and awarding bodies recommend that file copies be kept for three years before destruction. Records should be passed on promptly, as not doing this could hold up a candidate's assessment, especially if the observational assessor records form just part of a candidate's unit assessment. Records also provide the evidence for the sampling and monitoring activities carried out by the internal verifier, and hence must be kept up to date so that internal verification can take place throughout a candidate's progress.

(f) Follow the agreed complaints and appeals procedure if candidates do not agree with your assessment decision

Each organization should have its own complaints and appeals procedure, and both candidate and assessor should be familiar with this. In addition, awarding bodies will have their own complaints and appeals procedures, which should also be understood by candidates and assessors. These will be used if matters cannot be resolved locally.

7

Guide to Unit V1: Conduct Internal Quality Assurance of the Assessment Process

Unit V1 is for those who undertake the role of internal verifier for a centre. The internal verifier candidate will also be expected to be competent in assessing using a wide range of sources of evidence, and will have already obtained D33 or A1. The candidate should have practised as an assessor for a minimum of 12 months prior to undertaking the internal verifier role. The internal verifier role is a management function, and therefore is at NVQ level 4, unlike A1 and A2 (and D34), which are all at NVQ level 3.

The NVQ Code of Practice and the Joint Awarding Body (JAB) Guidelines are invaluable documents for internal verifiers (IVs). All IVs should be fully familiar with their contents and have discussed their implications with centre colleagues and assessors, and their external verifiers (EVs). All the explanations that follow should be read in conjunction with the JAB guide and the NVQ Code of Conduct.

There are four elements to V1:

- V1.1: Carry out and evaluate internal assessment and quality assurance systems.
- V1.2: Support assessors.
- V1.3: Monitor the quality of assessor performance.
- V1.4: Meet external quality assurance requirements.

V1.1: CARRY OUT AND EVALUATE INTERNAL ASSESSMENT AND QUALITY ASSURANCE SYSTEMS

(a) Put your organization's requirements into practice for auditing internal assessments and those of the external awarding body

A simple phrase that covers a lot of work! Organizations, particularly large organizations, have their own, often standardized procedures for auditing assessment. These need to be followed irrespective of any awarding bodies that may be involved with the centre. However, you will also need to ensure that the centre's procedures are acceptable to each awarding body with which you deal. The EV will expect you to explain the centre's systems and indicate why these meet the awarding body's specifications. You will have been given details of these specifications when the centre applied for registration. In rare cases, IVs may need to carry out some additional procedures to ensure that the awarding body's requirements are met.

You may need to liaise with others in the organization to obtain all the data you need. For example, in a large training organization there may be staff responsible for recruitment and enrolment with whom you need to liaise in order to get an idea of candidate numbers and expected timescale for completion. Similarly, you may need to give details of when you expect visits from the EV, and the status of the centre in terms of being able to make direct claims without waiting for an EV's visit.

It is your responsibility as the internal verifier to ensure that the requirements are acted upon, so you will need to show how you do this. Most IVs compile a centre file containing records of all the activity for which they are responsible.

(b) Identify the outcomes needed by the agreed standards and their consequences for internal auditing

The requirements of each NVQ will make resource demands on the organization. If there are too few qualified assessors or problems with centre Management Information Systems, for example, registration, assessment or certification could be held up. Most candidates will produce witness statements, and centres will need to have internal audit procedures for checking their authenticity, and sometimes for induction of witnesses. There will need to be safe and secure storage for candidate portfolios. Candidate assessors and verifiers will need to have all their decisions countersigned by qualified assessors. Sampling plans will need constructing and auditing, as will assessment tracking documents and assessment plans.

Where centres have been used to end-loading verification, and sampling only completed qualifications, practice will need to change to continuous sampling processes and cover all assessment activity, including observation, the assessment of independent assessors and of professional discussion.

(c) Carry out appropriate administrative and recording arrangements to meet external audit requirements

Previous EV reports should show how well the centre is doing in terms of administration and recording, and whether there are any current action points that the internal verifier should be following through. Current records will be needed to show that the necessary action is being taken. IVs need to be able to access relevant records on assessment practice and internal quality, and be able to give information swiftly. This information will include candidate/assessor allocation, sampling, tracking and standardization, numbers of registered, certificated and 'in progress' candidates, and the correct codes for courses, and will involve reviewing organizational policies to see whether they need updating with respect to assessment and verification.

(d) Identify the agreed criteria for choosing and supporting assessors, and ensure they are applied

The NTO assessment strategies for each NVQ will need to be matched to each assessor and IV. All those assessing and verifying A1, A2 and V1 will need to meet the assessment strategies of both the vocational awarding body and ENTO. You will need to be able to show that your records are regularly reviewed and updated. Since all awarding bodies require proof of relevant qualifications, a central file containing original certificates for vocational and assessor/verifier awards, with an accompanying CV, is very useful. If candidates do not wish their original certificates to be lodged with the centre, a photocopy endorsed by a qualified EV and the quality manager for the centre will be an acceptable substitute.

Each centre will have its own arrangements for supporting assessors, and these should be clear to all parties.

(e) Carry out assessment standardization arrangements

Carrying out assessment standardization arrangements will include holding meetings with assessors at which they all assess the same evidence, and assessors assess evidence from each other's candidates. Careful records need

---

- Library of documents, awarding body publications, QCA publications, training videos, books on assessment and quality assurance, supporting information on vocational NVQs offered
- Lists of training courses offered internally and externally
- Mentors for newly qualified assessors
- Programme of meetings for year, including general information, standardization and monitoring
- 'Buddy' system for qualified staff
- Monthly information sheet, containing updates on assessment practice
- Training needs analysis and continuing personal development plans for staff
- Written feedback on assessment decisions and observation monitoring

---

Figure 7.1 Some methods of supporting assessors

to be kept of attendees, the units sampled and the evidence used. Reports of the findings need to be made and distributed. The EV will want to see evidence of standardization activities related to assessment decisions.

(f) Ensure that a procedure for complaints and appeals is in place

The procedure for complaints and appeals must meet the requirements of the awarding body and must be followed where necessary. The organization's own complaints and appeals procedure needs to be checked against that for the relevant awarding body, to see whether any adjustments need to be made. There needs to be a clear procedure for recording complaints and their outcome, and how the organization or individual would action a complaint that needed referral.

(g) Identify and use internal and external measures of performance to adjust internal systems

The measures of performance are likely to be both quantitative and qualitative (Table 7.1).

Table 7.1 Some measures of quality

Quantitative measures	Qualitative measures
Numbers of enrolled, 'in progress', withdrawn and completed candidates	Availability of resources
	Policies and procedures
National benchmarking data for the qualification	Feedback from assessors and other centre staff
Time taken from enrolment to completion	External verifier reports on process
	Internal verifier or other internal quality reports
Audit trails checking compliance	
Data from satisfaction surveys	Reports from other examiners or inspectors
Records of complaints	
Equal opportunities monitoring data	Staff CPD records

(h) Make recommendations to improve internal quality assurance arrangements and develop a plan to put these improvements into practice

Having surveyed the data, both qualitative and quantitative, that are available to you, you need to summarize the information, preferably in both written and numerical/graphical formats. The report should be available for external auditors such as EVs and inspectors, as well as for internal quality managers. Its findings need to be shared with assessors in order to develop and maintain good practice, and determine the action that needs to be taken to maintain and/or improve performance.

V1.2: SUPPORT ASSESSORS

(a) Ensure that assessors have appropriate technical and vocational experience

Relevant and recent work-based experience is important for all assessors (and trainers), so work experience placements in industry, as well as training candidates in their vocational subjects, can help to keep assessors updated. This is particularly important for assessors who are based in colleges or training companies, who may spend much of the week away from the work environments attended by their candidates. Assessors of fast-moving vocational subjects such as engineering, IT or media will need to be familiar with technical developments in those areas.

In addition, assessors need to have a good range of information and communications technology (ICT) skills, so that they can take advantage of e-mail, electronic recording systems and information on the Internet from NTOs and awarding bodies. The ability to word-process, photocopy and scan material is now a key workplace skill, as is the ability to keep updated filing systems. The introduction of professional discussion, which must be recorded, means that assessors need to be able to use video equipment, audiotape equipment and possibly digital or other camera equipment. In addition, there are now IT-based initial assessment and diagnostic Key Skills packages that assessors can use at induction to enable them to give sound advice to candidates.

(b) Ensure that assessors are familiar with and can carry out the specific assessment and follow the recording and internal audit procedures

Centre induction will have provided assessors with the necessary initial information they need, including an introduction to the documentation and administrative systems they will be required to use. All assessors should have the opportunity to attend updating sessions, whether provided by the awarding body or cascaded through the internal verifier. You need to check that they have understood their training and are able to follow the systems. Keep records of your monitoring and of assessor attendance at training sessions.

(c) Identify the development needs of assessors in line with assessments, the needs of candidates and technical expertise and competence

Assessors can make self-assessments of their perceived needs that can be compared with the skills they need to perform their role. These can be checked against the requirements that the IV has identified as being mandatory and advisory to the centre's good quality practice, and action plans for each assessor drawn up on this basis. Most organizations have annual appraisals where individuals negotiate yearly action plans with their line managers. These may not cover the detail required here related to assessment, so the IV will need to conduct his or her own needs identification.

(d) Give assessors the chance to develop their assessment experience and competence and monitor their progress

Giving assessors this chance will require matching experienced assessors with those new to assessing itself, or new to assessing in a particular vocational area. Support may be required for all assessors as they work with the new A standards, until you are satisfied that they have successfully updated their practice. Keep records that show as a minimum who, how, what and when you have monitored concerning the assessment practice of your assessors. Experienced assessors may wish to explore new ways of recording assessment activity, such as by using digital equipment (PDAs) and online recording systems.

(e) Ensure that assessors have regular opportunities to standardize assessment decisions

There should be a planned timetable for assessors to get together to standardize their assessment decision. It might be helpful to plan the timetable so that there is always some standardization activity between EV visits, indicating who will be required to attend, so that assessors understand their commitments. Standardizing observation practice can be done using video evidence of candidates performing tasks, which can be viewed at leisure or alongside other assessors, and by having assessors complete assessment observation forms, and then reviewing them. Different types of portfolio evidence can be copied for assessing by a number of assessors, and a range of completed units can be assessed by different assessors, allowing differences and similarities in assessment practice, ways of giving written and oral feedback, and recording to be reviewed. It is also instructive to ask assessors to consider the minimum knowledge they require for the successful assessment of knowledge, by using a range of the questions in the standards and asking for written responses. Your standardization plan, attendance sheets and standardization reports from each session need to be available for quality assurance and EV scrutiny.

(f) Monitor how assessors are capable of maintaining standards

Your monitoring of assessors needs to be planned over time, so that you are confident that standards are maintained, and do not decline. It is equally important that both weak and over-rigorous assessment are addressed. You will do this through a combination of all your activities as an internal verifier.

V1.3: MONITOR THE QUALITY OF ASSESSORS' PERFORMANCE

The following criteria will be demonstrated by showing that you are checking that assessors are working to the A1 and A2 standards. You will need to work to these yourself in order to 'assess' the quality of the assessor performance for which you are responsible. Much of this work will be done through the implementation of your sampling strategy, where you monitor the assessment practice of assessors on a regular basis by dipping into assessments at all parts of the process. This will involve monitoring, for example, the assessment planning process with a newly registered candidate, as well as the monitoring of independent assessments, of observational assessors, and of final unit assessment and feedback to candidates. Sampling of finally assessed units is just one of the many parts of this process.

(a) Ensure that individual assessors are preparing for and planning assessments effectively

Ensuring that individual assessors are planning and preparing effectively can be done by viewing copies of assessment plans, and by talking to assessors, candidates and workplace supervisors. You will need to check that the assessor has considered the effectiveness in terms of both cost and estimated completion time of conducting the assessments. The separation out of training and assessment costs might need to be considered. The IV will need to monitor that assessors are making best use of workplace visits by well-planned assessments that cover a wide range of performance indicators, and that professional discussion is similarly effectively planned. The IV will also need to look at the use of observational and independent assessors, witness statements, postage costs, and the times taken by individual assessors to support candidates through to completion.

(b) Ensure that individual assessors have effective processes for making assessment decisions

You will need to check that assessors are assessing against the standards, rather than their perception of what is acceptable, and that their recording against criteria is done accurately and cumulatively. Candidates should know how much they have achieved from each assessment. These processes will be the ways in which individual assessors deal with the portfolio evidence, matching it to elements, performance criteria and knowledge, and checking their assessment against any claim the candidate may have indicated, prior to making their assessment. Assessors need to be supported to justify their decisions against the standards. Simple tick statements such as 'the evidence clearly meets the requirements' are not enough. The IV needs to be clear as to *why* the assessor believes this is so, and should be able to check the assessor's decision-making process and see exactly how the assessor has come to his or her decisions.

(c) Ensure that individual assessors understand the necessary outcomes

Assessors' understanding of the NVQ or unit requirements needs talking through. For example, there has been a perception that to get A1, an assessor needs to have seen a candidate through to successful completion of a unit. This is not so. The standard requires the candidate *to submit for summative assessment*; whether the candidate is judged competent or not yet competent is irrelevant.

(d) Ensure that individual assessors apply safe, fair, valid and reliable methods of assessing candidates' competence

The standardization activities you implement will help to ensure this, as will asking assessors to give verbal or written reports that indicate the measures they undertook to meet these criteria.

(e) Check individual assessors' judgements to ensure they are consistent over time and with different candidates

The checking process includes watching individual assessors carry out assessments and checking a sufficient number of assessors to ensure consistency between assessors over time and with different candidates. This is where you implement your sampling strategy, using the principles outlined in the JAB guidelines. A timetable of dates for sampling, with no strategy, is inadequate, as it is not linked into any programme of continuous improvement.

(f) Check a sufficient number of assessors to ensure consistency between assessors over time and with different candidates

Checking a sufficient number of assessors should not be a problem in centres with just a few assessors. In larger centres, the sampling plan will need to be robust enough to ensure that all assessors are making similar judgements against the standards, and that their judgements are not swayed by the particular needs of individual candidates. The IV needs to include all assessors, including independent assessors, in his or her sample. The IV should agree the sampling plan with the EV.

(g) Check different assessment sites to ensure that assessment decisions are consistent

It is important not only to sample documentary assessments from different sites, but also to visit different sites (e.g. sub-centres or satellites), as factors impinging on the assessments may not be apparent from the document without a visit. Resources, the nature of the candidates and the skills and experience of assessment staff can all affect assessment decision-making processes.

(h) Ensure that assessors set up and maintain effective working relationships with candidates at all stages of the assessment process

The key to ensuring effective working relationships will be assessment planning and review documentation, and any written feedback between candidate and assessor. More detail can be gained by contacting a sample of candidates, looking at any centre quality feedback forms, checking complaints, and reviewing assessment plans and feedback forms, particularly those on which the candidate responds to the assessor's feedback. Another measure of a good working relationship is the number of sound completions within the original estimated time that individual assessors achieve with their candidates. Slippage from this may indicate a misplaced reluctance on the part of the assessor to keep candidates to deadlines or to motivate candidates, or poor communications between candidate and assessor.

(i) Ensure that assessors apply relevant health, safety and environmental protection procedures, as well as equality and access criteria

Assessors must be aware of their responsibilities under the Health and Safety at Work Act, the Disability Discrimination Act, the Mental Health Act and the requirements in the Access to Assessment document published by the QCA. They need to show you how they have interpreted and applied these requirements, by providing themselves with the right clothing, conforming to the requirements of each particular workplace they visit, reporting situations of risk, and planning assessments to minimize barriers to access. The Data Protection Act will also need to be followed, as confidentiality regarding candidates needs to be maintained.

(j) Monitor how often assessment reviews take place and how effective these are

There must be a minimum of one assessment review per complete unit, but this is probably inadequate for all but experienced candidates. If assessors can indicate in their plans when they think reviews should be held, and keep records of whether these were implemented, monitoring should be fairly easy. It is important to separate out any meetings that assessors have with candidates that are focused on pre-assessment planning and training, either for the vocational NVQ or for the requirements for A1 and A2. Assessors occasionally get over-involved in support and training activities and fail to move candidates on in assessment.

(k) Monitor how often assessors give feedback to candidates and how effective this is

When sampling, IVs will look for written records that are signed and dated. It will be important to see whether candidates have acted on assessors' advice, and also whether the assessors are following through actions that they have asked candidates to undertake. If there is no evidence of written feedback in candidates' portfolios, the IV will need to check whether oral feedback is going unrecorded, and plan with the assessor how to formalize its recording.

(l) Monitor how accurate and secure assessors' record keeping is

Recording of achievement needs to be in duplicate. The candidate needs a copy, and the assessor needs a copy. Assessors' copies should be kept in such a way that they and others are unable to alter the documentation. Dating and signing all entries helps this process. Online systems prevent any changes to a candidate's evidence or an assessment decision once data has been entered.

(m) Give assessors accurate and helpful feedback on their assessment decisions

Moderating your decisions on an assessor with those of other IVs can help to reassure you that your decisions are sound, as can the feedback from your external verifier, or taking part in standardization exercises yourself. Feedback should be given in a way that enables the assessor to get credit for what he or she is doing well, and to act on any identified points for improvement that have been found to be needed. All feedback should be constructive.

V1.4: MEET EXTERNAL QUALITY ASSURANCE REQUIREMENTS

(a) Identify how internal assessments will be checked externally and the information needed for this purpose

The documentation received from the awarding body, together with previous external verifier reports, will provide guidance on this. Note the scheduled date of the next planned visit from the EV. You are likely to have to supply a range of material to the EV at least 15 working days before his or her visit. If the EV has not contacted you 30 days before the planned visit, it is advisable to contact him or her to confirm dates, times and what is wanted. Evidence of action to be taken by the centre following the last visit will definitely be required, as will details of any changes in the centre that affect assessment, such as new staff or assessment schedules.

If there is an internal verifier co-ordinator (IVC) for the centre, that person is likely to be the point of contact with the external verifier. You will need to liaise with him or her to check that you understand the part you will be playing in the process and what information will be required from you regarding the assessors for whom you are responsible.

(b) Plan, collect and analyse information on internal assessment decisions

You will need data from all the internal verification activity you have undertaken in the period since the last external verifier visit, assuming that the period you have taken to show your competence as an internal verifier has been at least this long so that your assessors have had time to develop through your monitoring processes.

It will probably be most helpful to present this information in a succinct, detailed written report, attaching any helpful data in the form of appendices. These might include lists of assessors and their candidates, tracking documents, or reports of standardization exercises. You could present data relating to the numbers of active and completed candidates for whom your assessors are responsible, and analyze the data looking for trends such as candidates who are slow to achieve. This may well lead you to take action in the form of supporting certain assessors to be more effective.

(c) Agree the timing and nature of external assessment audit arrangements

You will need to consult with your assessors and their candidates if the EV requests to observe assessment or visit assessment sites other than the main centre. Give estimates of the activities that are likely to be occurring, and check that staff will be available and how long centres will be open before confirming dates and times.

(d) Give supporting background information to external auditors about the assessment process

The EV will normally request exactly what he or she wants. An overall written report is very helpful, and shows that you are studying the results of your IV activity, are analysing what has happened, and are aware of actions that have been or need to be taken.

Your report can also highlight unusual circumstances that have arisen and affected assessment activity – for example, a large increase in the number of candidates following an award for excellence that has been won by the centre, or building activities or illness that has slowed down the assessment opportunities available to candidates.

(e) Explain any issues raised by external auditors and give them supporting information as necessary

During the external verification visit, you may be asked to supply missing or additional information, or to justify any of the documentation or decisions that you have supplied. All candidate portfolios not included at the last verification should be available for the verifier, so that he or she can take additional samples. This may involve asking candidates to bring in their previously assessed work, a process that you will need to start some weeks before the verification.

(f) Raise concerns and disagreements about external audit decisions in a clear and constructive way

External assessors may make decisions that indicate that practice needs improving in some way. If you have not supplied relevant evidence, or what you have supplied is open to interpretation, then their judgements may need to be revised in the light of additional evidence that you or others can supply. Disagreements and concerns are often resolved in this way. However, the EV may have identified areas for improvement that surprise you, and these need to be carefully clarified, bearing in mind that the EV should be able to justify his or her decisions against the NVQ Code of Conduct. This contains a table of sanctions (see Appendix 2), of which all assessors and verifiers should be aware. The EV should be pleased to advise you on how to meet the code if these are problems.

(g) Refer to the awarding body any questions or concerns that could not be dealt with internally

The centre contact or IVC (who may be different from yourself) is probably the best person to raise matters with the awarding body, which needs to limit, in a structured way, the contact with centres to ensure that key messages are transmitted to the right people. The 'awarding body' is likely to be, initially, the EV or the administrative centre.

(h) Give assessors feedback on external audit decisions

The centre will have a copy of the EV's report, either left at the time of the visit, or sent soon afterwards by the awarding body's administrative centre. The action plan from this needs to be available to all assessors. The IV will need to feed back to individual assessors who have had their decisions sampled, so that they are clear as to whether their judgements have been verified as correct, or whether they need to reassess any assessment decisions already made.

(i) Ensure that external auditing decisions are included in internal reviews of procedures

The organization needs to consider the outcomes of EVs' decisions, and show that it has taken these on board. Colleges and other training organizations supported via the Learning and Skills Council will need to incorporate the findings into the self-assessment report, so as an internal verifier you need to show that you know this has been done. Other organizations will have different reporting arrangements, but again they will need to show how the results have been communicated beyond the assessment team, and that they are part of the centre's overall review of quality.

8

Guide to Unit V2: Conduct External Quality Assurance of the Assessment Process

External verifiers are recruited and trained by awarding bodies. They are experienced assessors in their vocational areas. External verifiers of Learning and Development awards, which include the A&V awards, are also qualified and experienced in the area of Learning and Development. All external verifiers need to hold V2 or update from D35. Awarding bodies offer V2 to their verifiers.

External verifiers appointed to centres offering NVQs monitor and audit those centres to ensure that they are complying with the NVQ Code of Practice, the National Occupational standards being used, and the awarding bodies' own conditions of approval. They also offer support and advice to centre staff, and act as a channel of communication between centres, awarding bodies and lead verifiers.

Part of the monitoring role is to sample the centres' internal verification process. To do this, EVs need to sample all aspects of the internal verification and assessment systems. This means that an EV may need to attend standardization activities, accompany verifiers on observation visits, and talk to assessors or candidates, as well as verify that the assessment decisions made by assessors are accurate. They do *not* reassess candidates' work, and will sample only the work of candidates registered with the awarding body.

External verifiers normally act on a consultancy basis for their awarding body, and as such their work is part-time, on a daily basis.

V2.1: MONITOR THE INTERNAL QUALITY ASSURANCE PROCESS

(a) Monitor the organization's arrangements for auditing internal assessments.
(b) Plan and apply the monitoring procedures that the awarding body needs.
(c) Monitor how effective the chosen methods are against the necessary outcomes.
(d) Monitor how accurate internal administration and records are.
(e) Monitor the criteria used for choosing assessors.
(f) Recommend how the organization can comply with all relevant audit processes and procedures.
(g) Review how the internal assessment audit system is evaluated to ensure that the organization can comply with all processes and procedures.
(h) Give the awarding body accurate reports on the internal assessment process and any changes that may be necessary.

V2.2: VERIFY THE QUALITY OF ASSESSMENT

(a) Check to ensure that assessors and internal verifiers/auditors have the technical and vocational experience necessary to assess the agreed standards.
(b) Monitor the quality of induction and support procedures for assessors.
(c) Check that assessors have applied relevant health, safety and environmental protection procedures, as well as equality and access criteria, when carrying out assessment.
(d) Check the decisions made by a number of assessors to be sure that each is applying the assessment requirements consistently over time, with different candidates and in different parts if necessary.
(e) Get evidence of how effective working relationships between assessors and candidates are, along with assessment reviews.
(f) Review how accurate, prompt and secure individual assessors' record keeping is.
(g) Check that assessors have been given accurate and helpful feedback on their assessment decisions and performance.
(h) Identify concerns over assessors' decisions and review these with internal verifiers and auditors.
(i) Make a record of the results of the audit, using agreed procedures and documents.
(j) Agree and make a record of a course of action to put things right if assessment arrangements have not been satisfactory.
(k) Follow the agreed complaints and appeals procedure that the awarding

body needs if improvement and other related issues have not been sorted out.

(l)   Identify and highlight good practice and ensure you give positive feedback.

(m)   Give the awarding body full and accurate reports on the internal assessment process and any recommendations for changes to it.

V2.3: PROVIDE INFORMATION, ADVICE AND SUPPORT ON THE INTERNAL QUALITY ASSURANCE OF ASSESSMENT PROCESSES

(a)   Make early and regular contact with internal verifiers/auditors at all stages when developing assessment systems and procedures.

(b)   Identify concerns over the internal audit process and review these with internal verifiers/auditors.

(c)   Ensure that effective administrative arrangements are developed to support the internal audit and assessment process.

(d)   Agree how internal assessments will be externally audited, and the information needed for this purpose.

(e)   Give information and advice on the timing and nature of external audit arrangements.

(f)   Give the centre details concerning the people to be interviewed or involved in the audit process.

(g)   Identify and explain any issues concerning understanding of the awarding or accrediting body's criteria and requirements.

(h)   Raise concerns about internal audit procedures and assessment decisions in a clear and constructive way.

(i)   Give constructive and helpful feedback on external audit decisions.

(j)   Identify opportunities to improve internal audits and assessments, and give advice and support to help put these improvements into practice.

(k)   Carry out the appropriate complaints and appeals procedures if you are not able to resolve disagreements or concerns.

V2.4: EVALUATE THE EFFECTIVENESS OF EXTERNAL QUALITY ASSURANCE OF THE ASSESSMENT PROCESS

(a)   Identify and use internal assessment audit information to evaluate the systems and procedures of awarding bodies.

(b)   Contribute to the awarding body's standardization arrangements.

(c) Evaluate how effective the process of candidate assessment is as part of the internal quality assurance process, and report back to the awarding body and internal auditors.
(d) Review recording and administrative arrangements against information needed by the awarding body.
(e) Contribute to the awarding body's reviews of external auditing arrangements.

Part 3

Getting Your Award

Introduction: A Guide for A1, A2 and V1 Candidate-assessors and Candidate-verifiers

Where the pronoun 'you' is used in the text, it refers to candidate-assessors and candidate-verifiers. We refer to NVQs throughout as being the focus of assessment and verification practice. Assessors and verifiers of certain non-NVQ competence-based awards that have been submitted to and approved by the awarding bodies are also able to register for the Assessor and Verifier (A&V) units.

In Part 1 we have given background information on the organizations, the processes, and people involved in the assessment of NVQs. This should provide you with the requisite underpinning knowledge for the A&V awards.

Part 2 explains the performance criteria of the standards to which assessors and internal verifiers must work.

Now, Part 3 explores ways in which you may wish to approach your activities as a candidate-assessor or candidate-internal verifier, in order to gain certification yourself for the Assessor or Verifier awards. Before progressing with this section, we advise that you refamiliarize yourself with the A&V unit standards, as appropriate, and with those of your occupational area, eg Learning and Development, Beauty Therapy, Horticulture. If you are a candidate-assessor/verifier, it is imperative that you meet the occupational standards of the NVQ/mini-awards that you are assessing or verifying, and are familiar with the assessment strategy of the related NTO.

Candidate-assessors and candidate verifiers need to meet the assessment strategy for the NVQ that they will be assessing. This includes being qualified or well experienced in your specialist vocational subject, such as construction, health care or cleaning, prior to starting your A&V award. Access to bona fide candidates will also be needed. Candidate-assessors or verifiers who will be assessing or verifying Learning and Development NVQs, including those who may be assessing the A&V units as part of another vocational NVQ, need to meet ENTO's assessment strategy for Learning and Development. This includes competence in the vocational area of Learning and Development itself, and regular updating.

The process explained for you as candidate-assessors or verifiers will closely resemble the process that your own candidates will experience.

9

Preparing and Planning for Assessment

INDUCTION

As a candidate, you should receive induction from your accredited centre, where the requirements of the awards will be explained, and you will receive all accompanying documentation. You may be enrolled with the centre as a candidate at induction, and may even be registered for the award.

You should also receive details about the awarding body's complaints and appeals system, and have these explained to you. You should be clear at the outset of the verification and certification procedures involved in your assessment process, and of associated costs, particularly if there is an hourly, instead of a flat, rate for assessment. In other words, the assessment process you are to undertake as a candidate yourself should, like the assessment processes used with your own candidates, hold no surprises. Normally, your assessment will be 'continuous', as there will be a number of occasions on which you meet with your assessor for the purpose of checking work-based competence. There will also be a summative assessment when all your claims to competence are checked through, and the complete unit(s) are finally signed off.

You may be asked to complete a self-assessment of your Key Skills and of your current job role against the standards towards which you intend to work. This latter may take the form of a self-assessment checklist of your familiarity with performing tasks in each unit, and will help to identify whether you need any further training or experience before undertaking assessment.

The result of your induction may be an action plan that details things you need to do before presenting yourself for assessment.

Candidates must have either some identified candidates (for A1 or A2) or some assessors (for V1) with whom they are currently working. Simulation forms no part of the A&V awards. Until you are qualified, all your assessment or verification activity with your own candidates or assessors, including assessment decisions and documentation, will need to be countersigned by a qualified assessor or verifier. Sampling of countersigned assessments or verifications you undertake will be included in the centre's internal verification sampling plan, and you may be asked to be involved in standardization exercises. Your assessor *may* be qualified to countersign your vocational decisions, eg assessing care competencies as well as assessing assessment and verification competence. However, you may have a completely separate primary assessor to plan the assessment process for A1, A2 or V1 and to assess your unit, and you will need to get all your vocational decisions countersigned by a vocationally qualified assessor.

Independent assessment

You will also have an independent assessor, who will have no part in your assessment other than to assess 'a substantial part of the evidence'. This independent assessor may be from your own centre, but could be external to the centre. The awarding body will scrutinize the assessment decisions of independent assessors.

There are four methods of independent assessment allowed by the QCA. These are:

- have a visiting assessor;
- have tasks designed and assessed externally by the awarding body;
- have centre-devised tasks assessed by the awarding body;
- undergo another form of rigorous assessment acceptable to the regulatory authorities.

For the A&V awards, the independent assessor can decide what he or she wishes to assess. For the assessor awards, this is commonly one completed and reviewed assessment plan, drawn up between the candidate-assessor and his or her NVQ candidate. The independent assessor could, however, choose to assess knowledge and understanding, or even workplace assessment practice.

Unit for assessment: A1
Candidate: I Swilling
Primary Assessor: A Body

Methods agreed for assessment: observation, professional discussion, written questions, prior qualifications and experience, witness statements

Persons who will make assessments/judgements: A Body (primary assessor), B Kind (observational assessor), C Tuit (independent assessor, contact no 01234 567890, D Pending (candidate's line manager and witness), Z Carr (centre internal verifier)

Candidate-assessors vocational candidates, NVQ and units for assessment: E Longate, F Ahma, G Force all taking NVQ2 in Care
U 2   U 10   U 2

Process

Assessment Activity	Target Date
IS	
• To make unit plans with each of 3 candidates	
• To arrange with DP when they can be available for assessment	
• To contact BK and arrange observation date	by end of Week 1
• Conduct assessments with EL, FA and GF	by end of Week 5
• To ask DP for statement covering A1.3, A1.4	by end of Week 3
• To find vocational qual cert, cpd record	
• Complete answers to written questions relating to underpinning knowledge	
AB	
• To receive observational assessor report, witness statement, written answers, assess against standards, make judgement and provide feedback on one-to-one basis to IS	Thursday afternoon, 2–4 pm Week 6
• To update assessment plan and provide copy of assessment judgement and feedback to IS	(after week) in IS office
IS	
• To inform BK and AB when one of three candidates is ready for unit assessment	Week 8
• Arrange observation of unit assessment, and feedback to candidate; review assessment plan for candidate	
• Contact CT and arrange to send completed and reviewed assessment plan for assessment	Week 10
• Complete assessments with other candidates; arrange date with AB for workplace visit	Week 10
AB	
• Plan professional discussion and arrange loan of video camera	
• Visit IS in workplace; view evidence of three candidates; conduct professional discussion	Week 11 3 hrs
• Make assessment judgements, give feedback and review assessment plan; update tracking document	
• Arrange date for summative unit assessment	Week 12
IS	
• Organize portfolio of evidence and pass to AB for final assessment	
AB	
• Meet with IS at workplace for feedback; update assessment plan; pass result to ZC for results processing	Week 14 1 hr
	Estimated one-to-one time with assessor 8 hours
Signature Assessor Date	
Signature Candidate Date	time taken 1.0 hrs

Figure 9.1   A combined actions and assessment plan for an Assessor award

LOOKING AT YOUR OWN WORK CONTEXT

A useful starting point in the planning process to determine the strongest, most cost-effective ways of demonstrating competence, knowledge and understanding is to begin with your current place of work and job role. Consider the assessment planning and verification that normally take place within your own organization. This will enable you to build on what arises naturally from your own work instead of being tempted to manufacture an alien system of processes and procedures purely for the sake of achieving the award. In the past, candidates who have tried to do this have usually felt the assessment process to be mechanical paper gathering and have not understood or felt any ownership of the procedures involved. Unfortunately, this has sometimes resulted in some qualified assessors who have no belief in the quality of the assessment process. Those who have not found the process useful and meaningful themselves are unlikely to pass on much motivation or enthusiasm to their own candidates. Neither are they likely to understand the proper focus of NVQ assessment, which should be that of a range of ways of demonstrating competence, matched to the individual candidate, rather than a stereotyped approach to 'collecting evidence'.

As an assessor or verifier candidate, you might reflect on the process that your own assessor for the A&V units is taking with you. Are you encouraged to look at your assessment or verification practice as a way of maintaining or improving quality, and are you enabled to demonstrate your competence in ways that reflect the ethos of your own organization? Some useful questions to ask at this point are:

- How does assessment take place within my own work situation?
- How am I going to be involved?
- What procedures are already in place for monitoring and recording assessment?
- What are the procedures for verifying assessments?
- How do we usually test what someone knows and understands in my area of work?
- How do we check that candidates can operate in a range of situations and contexts?
- What guidance and planning takes place with candidates before assessment?

In order to individualize the process and enable it genuinely to reflect the assessment practice that arises from your own work situation, let us consider the different work contexts in which assessment might take place.

How does assessment take place in my own work situation?

Different work situations will sit more comfortably with different types of assessment. Although there will obviously be exceptions, it is likely that the following are fairly representative.

Schools and further education colleges

Schools and colleges of further education will have well-established assessment and verification systems, often biased towards written evidence from essays, tests or assignments. Assessments will be documented, and be part of a quality system that is subject to audit and inspection. Students are expected to achieve formal qualifications, and the achievement of Key Skills will be an integral part of the curriculum. Assessments will be academically or vocationally oriented. Commonly, 14- to 19-year-old students take NVQ programmes. Many college and school staff are trained as NVQ assessors and verifiers.

Large organizations

In most large organizations there will be well-established employee assessment systems. These may be linked to a staff appraisal system. These systems will be based on performance evidence, assessing how effectively individuals are carrying out their work roles and what the resultant training and development needs might be.

Formal appraisal systems will be documented, and there may be progress reports on individual employees, particularly those undergoing specific training. Informal assessments may be taking place on a continuous basis, particularly with trainees, and will probably take the form of a line manager or supervisor 'keeping an eye' on a trainee to see if he or she can do the job. In-house training may or may not be formally assessed. Employees may have been supported to obtain formal qualifications elsewhere. There may be strong NVQ systems in place – for example, hospitals train their auxiliary staff in customer service and care.

Small organizations

Smaller organizations will probably have continuous informal assessment of employees, based on performance evidence – that is, how someone is actually doing his or her job. For example, the owner of a small garage with a new trainee mechanic will probably be working in the same work area as his candidate. He will make regular mental notes of what the trainee can or cannot do (ie the areas where she is competent or not competent), where she needs to be shown how to do something properly, and where she can be trusted to do something completely on her own.

Many small organizations do not document their assessments, and there is unlikely to be any formal assessment of their employees' performance. Obvious exceptions to this are where Modern Apprentices are taken on by the organization, and are working towards NVQs, or where employers give formal feedback to external staff who have candidates undertaking work experience at employers' premises. There may be frequent assessment activity. For example, care homes, garages, hairdressers or hotels are likely to have NVQ assessors visiting their premises to assess employees.

In small organizations, employees may have been supported to obtain a formal qualification elsewhere, perhaps on a day-release basis. From these descriptions you will probably be able to identify the situation nearest to your own. You can then ask yourself the next question.

How am I going to be involved?

Assessor-candidates should be fully familiar with the practice of their centre, have bona fide candidates or assessors who are registered with that centre, and be a part of the assessment or verification team for the centre. Centre staff should keep you updated in the assessment and verification practice required in your vocational area. You will not be in a position to start your practical progress towards achieving your own certification until you have been allocated your candidates, if you are an assessor-candidate, or your assessors, if you are a verifier-candidate (though if you are reading this book prior to assessing or verifying, hopefully you are confirming or extending your knowledge!).

You need to identify with your A or V unit assessor whether your part in the centre's assessment or internal verification activities is likely to fulfil the evidence requirements for all the relevant elements, performance criteria, range, knowledge and understanding without calling on any other sources of evidence. Whether you think there are a number of existing procedures or you think you are starting without a formal assessment structure, it might be useful to recall the stages of the assessment process given in Chapter 1 and identify what documents might be needed to record these stages. More details on some of these documents are given later in this chapter.

How am I going to be involved in monitoring and recording assessment?

You will need to comply with the procedures of your centre, and use their documentation. This will be recording the assessment progress of your candidates

(A1 or A2), or for reporting on the quality of assessment in your centre for those assessors for whom you are responsible (V1).

Stages of the assessment process: some useful sources of information and reference for assessors

- *Planning for assessment:* awarding body guidelines, details of units and elements being covered, individual learning plans, interview or tutorial records, action plans, centre assessment strategy, assessment plan pro formas, assignment briefing sheets, internal verifier sampling plans, handouts giving guidelines to NVQ candidates, details of assessors/verifiers/witnesses, centre and satellite details.
- *Demonstrating competence:* candidate assessment plans, standards for relevant units or elements, witness authentication records, workplace practice and products, observation checklists, bank of questions, tests to show skills.
- *Making judgements:* awarding body guidelines, relevant standards, assessment plans, records of standardization events with other assessors to ensure consistency in judgements, recorded evidence from candidate, assessment criteria, feedback from internal verifier on assessor judgements, APEL evidence.
- *Giving feedback:* completed observation records, recorded or written evidence from questioning and professional discussion of candidates about their underpinning knowledge, completed feedback and tracking pro forma – formative and summative.
- *Recording decisions:* summative assessment sheets, candidates' log books, assessment tracking documents, overall summary sheet of units achieved, awarding body documentation recording candidates achievements, feedback from internal verifier, feedback from quality co-ordinator or administrator.

If the system operating in your workplace appears to have 'gaps' in practice or in documentation, you will need to discuss these with the relevant person in your workplace, such as your supervising assessor, your internal verifier or your quality co-ordinator. The Joint Awarding Body (JAB) Guidelines have examples of documentation, and explain clearly the assessment and internal verification processes that should be used.

What are the procedures for verifying assessments?

Organizations with verification systems are likely to administer and record them in different ways. However, all centres registered to run NVQs must comply with the NVQ Code of Practice, as well as with the relevant awarding body procedures. Their systems should have been agreed with the relevant external verifier. Assessors and internal verifiers should all have access to a copy of the awarding body's guidelines and a copy of all the units and elements which the assessors verify, the NVQ Code of Practice and the JAB Guidelines as a minimum. As a candidate-assessor or candidate-internal verifier, you need to ensure that you have this information before you start assessing, and that you give yourself time to read it before you start your work with candidates or assessors.

In what ways are knowledge and understanding tested within this work context?

The most natural method of testing knowledge or understanding is to question candidates or assessors while they are actually performing their tasks. This checks that they are clear what they are doing and that they have a proper understanding of what is involved. Additional discussions can take place, in which the candidate or assessor is questioned further, perhaps to elicit ideas on what they would do if a particular situation occurred, or if they had to perform the work in a different context – in other words, extending the scope of the task, and covering a variety of contingencies.

There is a contrast between this work context and one such as a school or a college, where some form of written testing would be part of the normal expectations of being in such an environment. Although oral testing on an ongoing basis would be part of the process of formative assessment, most students would expect to have to prove knowledge and understanding through written means at various points in the programme. When deciding the most appropriate ways of testing, it is therefore important to consider what is most cost-effective to your own candidates, and formulate ways of testing that are most likely to elicit answers that provide a genuine reflection of what they know and understand.

Certain awarding bodies for NVQs do now specify at least one written test. The evidence on testing knowledge and understanding that you produce for your A1 awards might include one or more of the following:

- a bank of questions that you use for oral testing;
- examples of written tests that you use;
- examples of assignments or projects identifying the elements and perform-ance criteria being assessed;
- notes you have made on constructing tests and assessment schemes, or a record of professional discussion where such matters are explored in some depth.

Are the range or scope of situations covered?

Candidates for the assessors' awards are often covering all the range without realizing it, perhaps because they are not doing it consistently or systematically. For example, one assessor-candidate working in the vehicle body area did not think he was covering the range *candidate and peer assessment* because he was not doing this on a formal basis. However, he was asking his vehicle body candidates what they thought of their own work and he was getting other vehicle body candidates to comment on each other's work. Once this was pointed out to him, he began to do this in a more systematic fashion and to record the comments as they were made. The evidence was already there; he just needed to realize this and structure it more consistently. This also had the effect of improving his own assessment practice, as he made sure that everyone had the opportunity to give and receive feedback and ideas for improvements. Where not all the range is covered, you need to work out whether you would be able to cover the range by reorganizing your work, eg by 'swapping' candidates with a colleague. If not, then you should discuss with your adviser or assessor the most appropriate way you could demonstrate specific aspects of the range, possibly by answering a number of pre-set questions, eg 'What if. . .?' questions.

What guidance and planning takes place with candidates before assessment?

Do centre assessors model good practice in planning assessments themselves by taking candidates through the processes described earlier in this chapter? Do they confirm holistic assessment plans for each NVQ unit they are taking, preferably using observation and professional discussion as the primary assessment methods? We have known many cases where assessment planning by Learning and Development assessors is often weaker than that between candidate-assessors and their NVQ candidates!

THREE METHODS OF DEMONSTRATING COMPETENCE

Observation of work-based performance

Observation of work-based competence will be the primary source of evidence for your competence and knowledge. (There are only 17 performance criteria in the Learning and Development standards that do not need to be observed.)

It is evidence that you are currently able to perform particular aspects of a role within an occupational area, witnessed and recorded against performance criteria by an accredited assessor observing you actually carrying it out. It can also be the result of the 'performance', ie the product or products that result from performing the particular task or skill. These 'products' could be a manufactured article or a successfully completed installation or repair. Although 'product' is an impersonal term, an assessment for a candidate in an NVQ in child care and education working with a group of obviously happy and well-cared-for children would take into account the successful 'products' of the work he or she is performing. The products you might produce could be documents you have used for recording interviews or tutorials, and also planning sheets, evaluation sheets, etc.

The best kind of performance evidence is that which arises naturally from your work situation. There may be a limited number of occasions where simulation in the form of specially designed tasks or role plays is necessary, eg in a situation where a candidate might have to demonstrate competence in emergency procedures. For those working towards the A&V awards, simulation is no longer allowed. This is to ensure that the awards are given only to those who have demonstrated that they have met all the standards through normal work duties. Candidates need to show that they can carry out assessments with all the pressures and constraints of real assessment practice, which includes the skill of forming a constructive relationship with the individual whom they are assessing. The best safeguard in relation to simulation is to consult with external verifiers and the awarding body for guidance.

In the A&V awards, as in other awards, as much evidence of your competence and knowledge as possible should be generated through that provided by being directly observed and questioned while carrying out your role. It will fall to your supervising specialist vocational assessor or internal verifier to do much of this. These observations will be supplemented by a professional discussion between you and your A or V assessor, where underpinning knowledge and application of the performance criteria in the work situation can be considered and elaborated upon. Much of your 'evidence' therefore, will consist of the records made by your own assessor.

Supplementary evidence

As one would expect, supplementary evidence is evidence to supplement any gaps in the performance criteria not met through direct observation and questioning and/or professional discussion. Most observations will include questioning to show that you have the required knowledge and understanding. This can be provided through your assessor asking you a series of questions, by having to sit a written test or by writing an explanation of your understanding of a particular process or area of knowledge. Candidate-internal verifiers may record an account of what they understand by verification and how verification works within their own organization. Candidate-assessors may wish to convince their official assessor that they have good background knowledge of assessment, so they may include a description of different types of assessment they have used in the past, together with some evaluation of their strengths and weaknesses.

The place of prior achievements or prior experience in demonstrating competence

There are a number of different sources that are valid forms of evidence. Letters, witness statements, or reports from third parties on work in which you have had direct involvement are valid only if they indicate with precision the types of activities you have been carrying out effectively, so that these claims of your competence can be matched to the relevant performance criteria in the standards. One candidate whom we assessed had been working in a glass-making factory and had been involved in producing a large report involving assessment of health and safety procedures within his workplace. Assessor-candidates could produce third-party evidence from a recent external verifier's report which showed that their own assessment practice was accurate, or a line manager's report witnessing that they had been on relevant updating programmes and had planned continuous professional development (CPD) activities for the coming year related to their vocational area. Evidence can also be provided from certificates and qualifications gained in the past proving that you have the relevant experience and competence.

However, in all these cases the *currency* of competence is the all-important factor, and if there is any doubt of your ability to perform to current national standards then your assessor will probably want to observe you directly to confirm that you really are competent.

Prior achievements, particularly where you have done written work such as essays or assignments or produced training materials, are often useful for supplementing the knowledge and understanding required. An assessor-candidate who had completed an initial teacher or trainer training qualification such as the Certificate in Education for the post-16 sector should certainly have covered assessment during those programmes and may have kept written evidence of that fact. His or her assessor would need to check that the assessor-candidate could apply this prior knowledge to the NVQ situation.

BEING QUESTIONED

Irrespective of your position and experience, being questioned by an assessor can still be a stressful occasion, if only because you may be highly practised and knowledgeable, and thus you will be *expecting* to be deemed competent!

The assessor may ask you to describe or explain your evidence, so refer to any product- or paper-based evidence to save time. Often the focus will be on exploring how much knowledge is covered by the activities that the assessor has seen you carry out in workplace practice, or asking you what pc/pi or range you think are met by some of your evidence. The assessor should, following good assessment practice, have a pre-prepared list of questions from which an appropriate selection is made, and should record your answers. See Chapter 2 for help on devising questions to check underpinning knowledge and understanding. Figure 9.2 gives a sample list of questions for use with an A or V assessment of natural performance.

---

1. How had this assessment been agreed with your candidate?
2. What determined the physical arrangements, eg where you stood, when you asked questions?
3. What did you do to encourage the candidate to select and present relevant evidence?
4. How did you decide/construct the questions you asked orally? Are the questions written down?
5. What is your definition of a 'leading question'? How can you avoid asking them?
6. Why did you ask the number of questions that you did?
7. How are you sure that you can infer competent performance in other situations where the task/activity might occur?
8. In what ways can you involve candidates in their own assessments? How effective was the candidate's performance in this case? How might it be improved?
9. What rules do you follow when giving feedback?
10. How do you encourage individuals to ask questions as a natural part of the feedback and evaluation process?
11. What makes this assessment fair, reliable, valid and sufficient?
12. Did this candidate have any special needs for which you had to cater? What special needs might candidates have and how would you accommodate these?
13. Are there any aspects of my assessment of you about which you are unclear, or which you wish to discuss further?

Figure 9.2 Sample questions for use with assessment observations

Some questions might be of the 'closed' variety, particularly if the assessor is checking fact, eg 'What was the tolerance on that measurement?' Others are likely to probe processes, such as 'How did you help the teacher to plan that work?', or 'What is the basis on which you have drawn up your sampling plan?'

You might be asked such questions immediately after assessment of your performance, or in a summative assessment check, if the assessor is unclear as to whether performance and supplementary evidence meet all requirements.

If you have had the opportunity to work through similar lists of questions beforehand (for assessment techniques and for underpinning knowledge and understanding), you could include your answers as supplementary evidence, as doing so may save unnecessary oral questioning. On the other hand, you may prefer to prepare the answers mentally and answer oral questions rather than put a lot down in writing. The assessor will also be determining the authenticity of your evidence; this is particularly important where you might have been working as part of a team and where there may be some 'common' evidence. If this is the case, it is really important that you are clear about why the evidence demonstrates your competence, rather than that of the team itself or of another team member.

You should of course receive constructive feedback after any assessment. Most assessors will give this verbally, but usually there will be an additional written report confirming satisfaction with the evidence, or detailing where competence has not been fully shown.

Assessments can vary considerably as regards time taken. The variation has been due to the *amount* of evidence presented, the *nature* of the evidence (an assessor may choose to look at the whole of an assessment recorded on video, in addition to other performance evidence), the overall grasp of the assessment process shown by the candidate, and the candidate's ability to respond concisely to the details needed. 'New' assessors frequently take longer to complete the assessment process, owing to a variety of factors, not least of which can be the lack of co-ordinated planning of assessment opportunities in the workplace and the impulse to encourage candidates to unnecessarily include additional material 'to be on the safe side'.

SPECIFICATIONS, SOURCES OF AND PURPOSES OF EVIDENCE

Always select evidence of performance and knowledge that shows the consistency of your activity over time. Any evidence must meet the requirements of authenticity, validity, reliability and currency (see Chapter 3). The following list, although by no means comprehensive, may provide you with some ideas on the variety of evidence you can use to demonstrate competence as an assessor or internal verifier both from present work roles and from previous experience or achievements:

Evidence	Purpose is to:
action plans	show details of initial assessment and review with candidates

Table 9.1　Advantages and disadvantages of different types of evidence

Source of evidence	Assessed by	Advantages	Disadvantages
Natural performance	Direct observation of you at work Examining end product	Current Can cover range of elements and performance criteria if planned well Convenient (if part of your normal work) No problem with authenticity if you are actually seen performing	Can be costly in assessor time if assessor and candidate work in different places; special arrange-ments to fit in with your assessor's availability may be needed; you may perform less well owing to 'nerves'; possibly disruptive to colleagues
Specially set tasks or situations	Simulations • Role plays • Assignments • Projects etc Professional discussion	Current and live Enables you to demonstrate competence in performance criteria or knowledge not easily shown in other ways Controlled situation or task	Can be difficult to construct a realistic situation; you may under perform because the situation is artificial; tasks, projects and discussions need meticulous planning to ensure candidates cover the required criteria; technical issues, eg video
Questioning	Oral tests Written tests Essay questions Full assignments or projects	Can be a quick way to provide evidence; can support other evidence by providing context and depth; oral questioning can be done as part of the observation; written tests can cover broad spectrum	You may be nervous at being 'tested'; you may misunderstand the questions; you may have to use written skills that are not necessarily appropriate to your competence at work
Historical and third party	Evidence from prior experience,	Can save time, if you have wide variety of	The evidence may not be current for

Table 9.1 Continued

Source of evidence	Assessed by	Advantages	Disadvantages
	achievement or learning Witness statements and testimonials	relevant experiences and have them well documented and organized; can provide evidence of knowledge and understanding; can provide evidence of range not covered by current situation	today's working standards; matching it against the standards could be more time-consuming than demonstrating competence in other ways; may be difficult to prove that it is authentic; may take time to source evidence

APL documents	show previous competence/experience and, by inference, current competence
appraisal records	indicate activities undertaken or planned that meet CPD requirements of assessment strategy
assessment plans	show compliance with A1.1
assignments (marked)	show knowledge and understanding related to units
audiotapes	referenced to recording of questioning or professional discussion between assessor and candidate
briefing notes to staff	show that relevant information is communicated
candidate tracking docs	show regular recording of assessment decisions
certificates (original)	provide evidence of relevant qualifications
costings (time, money)	to show understanding of efficiency
data print-outs	provide information for external verifiers and quality assurance
feedback sheets to candidates	constructive feedback given at appropriate times
forms, pro forma	correct inputting of necessary information
graphs	to show analysis of quantitative data
individual learning plans	assessment planning and reviews with candidates
induction documents	provide focus for explaining how they are used with candidates/staff
job specifications	discuss with assessor at registration/evidence of meeting assessment strategy
memos	show communication
minutes of meetings, eg standardization	show contribution and attendance of assessors

photographs	show artefacts/products that assessors are not able to view themselves
policies and procedures	provide focus for explaining how policy impacts on own practice
questions, written or oral	use with candidates to test knowledge and understanding, answers logged and recorded
record sheets	show ability to track, eg monitoring of assessors
reports	(qualitative) show how activities have been carried out, evaluate
reports (quantitative)	give summary of data derived from analysis
review sheets	show monitoring of assessment progress with candidate
sampling plans	to indicate monitoring activities
staff lists	fair and considered allocations for verifier: assessors, and assessors' candidates
verifiers' reports	show how assessor or verifiers' assessment decisions have been sampled, and the results of sampling activity
videotapes	provide evidence of professional discussion or workplace performance
witness statements	validated performance and product evidence not seen by primary or observational assessor
workplace performance	competence against majority of performance criteria

YOUR ASSESSMENT PLAN

You should not be put in the position of negotiating and agreeing your assessment plan before you are fully familiar with the process for your awards, and for your centre's operation of its NVQs and their assessment and verification. Once you are fully familiar with your centre's processes, and have completed any necessary training or practice, you are ready to begin your own assessment process, and agree your assessment plan. Your first assessment planning meeting with your primary assessor should give you an overview of how the assessment for the whole award is envisaged, and should result in the detailed planning for the assessment of at least one complete unit.

The negotiated plan will cover the (minimum of four) methods that will be used to assess your knowledge and competence, what you will need to do or present to demonstrate knowledge and competence, what this will involve, who will be involved, and the planned timescale. Each plan should cover at least one NVQ unit, as indicated in the agreed common evidence requirements (see Chapter 3).

Table 9.2 Simple action plan following the findings of initial assessment for an A2 candidate

Areas of competence	Identified training needs
Start to collect evidence of: • Prior activities • Relevant original certificates • CPD records for last year re quals and assessment updating • Witness statements against relevant criteria • Observing Candidate A for Unit 4 of NVQ 2 in ABC • My assessment decisions for Candidates A and B • Etc. . .	• Read up on setting tests and marking assignments • Find out how to update tracking sheets on to centre's electronic system • Talk to IV about inclusion of my assessments in sampling plans • Read up on HASAW and Data Protection Acts • Practise using video recorder when observing and questioning candidates • Etc. . .

You will end up with two sets of plans. The first set will be those you have drawn up with your assessor that cover A1, A2 or V1. The second set of plans will cover, if you are a candidate-assessor, the assessments you plan to make of your own NVQ candidates, and, if you are a candidate-internal verifier, the plans that will show how you will carry out your role with your allocated assessors.

THE NEXT STEP

It is now up to you as the candidate-assessor or candidate-verifier to put the assessment plan into practice. If you have bona fide candidates, and are linked into your centre's internal verification process, there should be few problems, barring those caused by illness, or disruption to work activity outside of your control. You will need to make sure that all the people identified in your plan are aware of their part in your assessment. Ensure that your workplace assessor knows how to contact you and locate you. If he or she is not part of your own organization, make sure that the assessor receives any necessary health and safety induction prior to carrying out workplace assessments. Keep to agreed times, and sign and date any reviews or assessment feedback then and there. Make sure you have copies of your assessor's decisions and feedback on your performance, and that you are clear on what you have achieved at all times during the process.

One-to-one assessment is a costly business. Keep chat to a minimum, and if you find that you need more time to read up on skills, or get more experience, discuss this with your assessor, and review your plan.

SUMMARY

This chapter should have helped you with:

- pre-assessment activities;
- induction and self-assessment;
- looking at your own work context;
- three methods of demonstrating competence;
- specifications, sources of and purposes of evidence.

10

Tips for a Stress-free Process for Demonstrating Your Competence

This chapter aims to assist assessor and verifier candidates to move to certification as swiftly as circumstances allow. The advice from the QCA is to use a wide range of evidence, and get away from the collection of paper evidence. The best way to do this is to take a process-based, rather than a product-based approach to assessment. In other words, the focus should be on assessing the candidate-assessor/verifier in the workplace, rather than the candidate producing huge files of documentation.

PROCESS

You and your primary assessor will have decided the ways in which you are going to undertake to demonstrate competence, and these will be detailed in your assessment plan. Much of your evidence will come directly from your primary or observational assessor, in the form of assessment observations or reports on your activities as a candidate. Your evidence and your assessor's decisions on it may be requested for sampling by your centre's internal verifier, so you should ensure that any feedback and recording of results given to you by your assessors, and the assessment plan with any reviews, are available with your own materials.

The assessment plan you agree with your assessor should set out all the necessary details, including target assessment dates, and arrangements for reviews. Keeping to the timescale envisaged will be the first thing that you can do to help your assessment be an enjoyable experience for yourself, your own candidates or assessors, and even your primary and independent assessors!

THE PORTFOLIO

As you progress through your awards, you will use and receive a number of documents and products such as assessor reports and feedback on your performance, video- or audiotapes of the professional discussion, or photographs or samples of your own candidate's achievements. This evidence of your competence as an assessor or verifier candidate is normally presented for assessment in a referenced file, folder or box, usually termed a 'portfolio'.

A familiar example of a portfolio is that of the art student who has a varied collection of samples of work. Items that are inappropriate for folder presentation, such as sculpture or ceramics, are often represented by photographs, or by written reference to their location if, for example, they have been sold. Other examples are an actor's portfolio, representing the range of roles played, and the portfolios held by cabinet ministers, which are the range of activities and responsibilities expected of them.

Your own portfolio is likely to be a collection of mixed evidence, much of which may not be in written form. Most candidates opt to keep necessary documentary or small product evidence in a binder containing plastic wallets. If you are submitting for a number of units, a separate (floppy) binder for each unit can be useful. An A4 lever arch file is unwieldy and normally far too large for the documentary evidence required for A&V awards.

Many documents should never be put in the portfolio, but will be viewed *in situ* in a candidate's workplace, and be acknowledged through assessor reports of assessed activities including video and photographic evidence. Candidates commonly include irrelevant or superfluous materials. Not only do these take up unnecessary space, but also they alert the assessors or verifiers to the fact that you may be unclear as to what constitutes relevant evidence. You could therefore be advising your own candidates poorly and encouraging them to think that the process is about chasing paper rather than performing jobs in an informed way to particular standards.

Review each item of evidence or process you identify as demonstrating your competence or knowledge and ask yourself:

- Does this relate to my assessment plan?
- Is this evidence relevant to the unit(s) and, if so, to which element(s)?
- Does the evidence demonstrate competent performance, have I explained the context in which the tasks are done, and/or does it demonstrate underpinning knowledge or understanding?

- If it does, how am I going to explain or indicate to my assessor what competences or knowledge I am claiming?
- Is the evidence recent and authentic – in other words, does it prove that I am currently competent?
- Do I have sufficient examples of meeting performance criteria over time?
- Does this evidence need to be physically included in my portfolio, or would it be better to show it to my assessor during or following an observation, or during professional discussion?

If you are unsure, get advice from your assessor. The standards now give clear guidance as to the agreed evidence that you must show to your assessor, and if you follow this guidance you should have no problems with sufficiency or validity.

Remember: one of the signs of good assessors, or candidates, is that they are able to identify *relevant* evidence that covers as many performance criteria as possible. There is *no* positive correlation between large paper-based portfolios and good assessor or verifier practice!

PAPERLESS PORTFOLIOS

There are now computer-based recording systems on the market that enable the assessor to capture all assessment activity on-screen. All necessary recording pro formas are online. Candidates' work may be scanned into the electronic system, and assessment and verification records can be entered straight into it. Feedback comments can be sent online to candidates. Internal and external verifiers can access the system at any time to verify assessment activity.

The paperless portfolio is, like any recording system, as good as those using it. Like a paper-based system, it relies on the assessor or internal verifier to enter data regularly.

Perhaps the best 'paperless portfolio' is that which is focused on well-planned workplace observations, witness testimony and professional discussion. An assessor who spends time in the candidates' workplace talking to witnesses, seeing activities and looking at the outcomes of that performance, and records what the candidates have achieved in detailed but concise statements matched to the standards, should not need the candidates to collect any 'paper evidence'. The assessor's reports should provide a sufficient audit trail of the candidates' competence.

SAVING YOUR TIME

The major factors influencing the time you take to get your award are likely to be the following:

- *The support, advice and documentation provided by the awarding body with which you register.* Make sure you have a registration number from the awarding body as soon as you have been identified as a suitable candidate for an award. You will have to wait a minimum of 10 weeks from registering for your awards before you can be entered for certification. This is known as the '10-week rule'. Check that you have a full copy of the occupational standards, and any helpful materials provided by the awarding bodies. The awarding body's and ENTO's Web sites will be helpful here (see the list of further reading at the end of the book).

- *The support, advice and documentation provided by the centre with which you enrol.* Check out the amount of time your centre has allocated for your support, and plan with your assessor at the outset how it will be used. Keep appointments, and let your assessor know in good time if you need to cancel visits. Ask what additional support the centre can provide, such as computing or library facilities. Ensure that you have access to the NVQ Code of Conduct and the JAB Guidelines, and the document 'Access to Assessment'. Reading these will help you to get an understanding of the issues around assessment and internal verification, and give you a broader perspective than that of your centre or awarding body. Ask if you have any queries.

- *Your familiarity with your vocational standards.* Discuss these with other assessors at your workplace, and get advice from your vocational internal verifier if you need to. If you are an A1 or A2 candidate, decide which units are likely to be most quickly achievable by your own candidates, as you need to assess completed (but not necessarily satisfactory) units before you can get your own qualification.

- *Your familiarity with the assessment and/or internal verification process.* The more experience you have of this and the more closely you are integrated into the centre's operation, the easier it will be to undertake the process as a candidate. You will need to ensure that your own internal verifier is including you in standardization activities, and that you are able to carry out all the activities required by the standards. No simulation is allowed. If this is a problem, you need to take advice, as the A&V awards may not be appropriate for you, or alternatively your centre may need to review its processes if it wishes you to achieve.

- *The progress of your own NVQ candidates or your assessors.* The speed with which your own candidates progress will affect your own ability to complete quickly. You have to be in a position to assess a complete unit for at least two candidates for A1, and have those assessments built into the internal verification system. For V1, you will need to be in a position to meet with your assessors regularly, and have regular contact with your supervising internal verifier. You also need to be able to participate in the centre's quality assurance process, and make reports to key people, so you need to know when the centre conducts its audits, and how your verifications will link with the centre's external verification process.

- *The support of your workplace colleagues as, for example, witnesses or vocational observers.* Assuming that your centre has suggested that you get the award, then hopefully the staff will be fully behind you, and prepared to carry out observations or verify your practice as required. Even so, staff may well need to meet with you initially so that they are clear about your expectations. If you are taking the certificate for other reasons, you need to think carefully about who you will need to work with in the centre, their own work commitments, and what you can do to see your award as useful to the centre and themselves.
- *Your commitments in and outside work.* However well you plan, the unexpected always happens, so it can be worth thinking through some contingency plans if, for example, your candidates leave unexpectedly, or there is a crisis at home. Ensure that you let your assessor and others who may be affected know as soon as possible in case they are able to help.
- *Your ability to select and present evidence clearly.* If you understand the standards, and can see that they represent a job broken down into its constituent parts, you will find it easier to select assessment opportunities that cover substantial parts of your required performance. The clarity with which you are able to link your evidence to performance criteria, range/ scope and knowledge, the easier it will be for your assessor to make the necessary judgements. Your assessor should be looking to see that you have confidence in your role, and that you understand what you should be doing and how you should be working.

ACCESSIBILITY AND LEGIBILITY

There are no rules regarding the way that your evidence should be organized, or the order in which it should be presented. Assessors will need to be able to tell what part of the assessment plan evidence they are reviewing, and internal verifiers will need to be able to find copies of your assessors' judgements and feedback on your evidence. This applies to practical activities and discussions you have, as much as to documentation. Your awarding body or centre may have specific pro formas, such as assessment plans or feedback sheets that you need to complete. Ensure that any dating, signing or countersigning of assessment observations, assessments or other documentation such as witness statements is done at the time the activities take place. The purpose of signing and dating is to confirm that certain activities happened at that particular time and place, between those particular people. If much of your evidence is on videotape, a brief written explanation attached to the cassette box will be helpful for anyone sampling the contents. You will need to think of a way of ensuring that the time of the recording and the identity of those on the tape are clear to your primary assessor, if he or she was not involved.

A professional approach is important, and any documents you complete should be legible and fit for purpose, and should conform to the Data Protection Act. Pro formas completed by hand while observing or interviewing candidates, or other types of working documents such as memoranda, should be kept in their handwritten state, as they are primary evidence. Retyping such evidence in not advised or necessary. However, all handwritten evidence should be legible, particularly if it is to be read by candidates or staff involved with the assessment process. If you have video, audiotape or digitally recorded material, the sound quality should be reasonable, and there should also be an index so that both you and the assessor can easily and quickly find specific items. Similarly, photographs need to be verifiable, and there are plenty of cheap cameras on the market that insert the date and time on to images. The way that you prepare your evidence and the documentation you use to record plans, assessments and feedback will probably be useful in helping you to develop a method and standard of evidence building that can be a model for your own candidates or assessors.

See Table 10.1 for the evidence requirements for A1 and A2.

FORMATS FOR PRESENTATION FOR SUMMATIVE ASSESSMENT

Sometimes centres will ask candidates to put their evidence together in a particular way. If this way does not suit you, then be prepared to say so. Assessors, internal and external verifiers should be checking your evidence against the standards, not against any pre-prepared format. If you need some guidance, the following points may be helpful:

- Label your 'portfolio', whether a file, wallet or box, clearly, with your name, the units you are claiming and your organization (if relevant).
- Put a contact number or address with your evidence.
- A chart that shows your relationship to your candidates/assessors and your line managers is helpful for an internal verifier who might be sampling the assessments made on your evidence.
- Witness statement sheets with sample signatures, including those of everyone who has contributed to your assessment, will help your assessor with his or her judgements, and the internal verifier if your work is sampled.
- Provide a list of the evidence being used for your summative assessment, with any reference numbers. This list should also include evidence that has been reviewed by your assessor at your workplace, and is therefore not included in your portfolio. Include the location of any such evidence (eg filing cabinet, display board in classroom).
- Include the assessment plan signed by you and your primary assessor, reviewed as necessary.

Table 10.1 Evidence requirements for A1 and A2

A1 assessor	A2 observational assessor

• A minimum of two candidates
• Three assessment plans, each covering one full unit of competence, which have each been reviewed and updated
• Minimum of four assessment methods to be used to assess evidence across three plans
• One written or spoken explanation (recorded) explaining why the four assessment methods have been chosen, why they are valid, reliable and fair, and precisely who and how others have been involved
• Three assessment decisions for a minimum of the two candidates identified in the assessment plans
• One record of observation and feedback to one of the identified candidates
• Two records of feedback provided on two other occasions, with written records of observation, or endorsement by, an experienced assessor from a registered centre
• One record (ideally taped or video-recorded at the candidates' workplace) of professional discussion, which can cover the explanations needed for all four elements, ie
  1. *developing plans*
  2. *judging at least three different types of evidence*
  3. *the use of observation*
  4. *the implementation of assessment methods*
  5. *the evaluation of effectiveness of the method*
	• A minimum of two candidates
	• Three assessment plans, each covering one full unit of competence, which have each been reviewed and updated
	• Two written progress reviews for two candidates
	• Evidence of having updated assessment plans and outcomes of review
	• Three assessment decision records relating to the three assessment plans, for the two candidates
	• Professional discussion (recorded) where candidates present how they have: 1) used observation of performance to demonstrate achievement of particular standards; 2) evaluated the effectiveness of the assessment methods in the light of assessing candidates
	• Three assessment decision records for at least two of the three different assessment plans for A2.1
	• Record of professional discussion to show how candidate has: 1) used questioning to demonstrate the knowledge requirements; 2) evaluated the effectiveness of the assessment methods in the light of assessing candidates
	• Minimum of one observation by the assessor of the assessor candidate providing feedback to one candidate
	• Evidence of feedback on two other occasions – written records for endorsement by another recognized assessor

Table 10.1 Continued

A1 assessor	A2 observational assessor
6. *the demonstration of competence in relation to criteria c, d, g* 7. *providing feedback and support relating to criteria a, d, f* • Two assessment records, one for each of two different candidates • Two instances of reviewing candidate evidence (two pieces of evidence for two different candidates), which *must* have contributed to the internal standards procedure • One written statement from the person responsible for internal verification and monitoring, showing how the assessor has contributed to agreed quality procedures	• Assessment methods for two different candidates which have been passed to the IV (or QA person) • Written statement from IV to show that assessor has contributed to agreed QA procedures

- Include record(s) of professional discussion.
- Include written feedback from your assessor.
- Include a copy of your assessor's tracking document showing your progress.
- Provide copies of assessor decisions on your competence.
- Include any supplementary evidence not yet seen by your assessor, but which the assessor needs in order to make a final decision.
- Ensure that everything is secure, and that nothing is likely to fall out or drop off.

Leave out:

- Original certificates or photocopies, unless your assessor has not checked and noted these at the beginning of the process.
- Any pro formas, eg assessment feedback forms, that have not been completed appropriately.
- Any materials you have been given as part of your training.
- Any paperwork or documents that are not clearly related to your competence.

- Any paperwork or documents that are not clearly related to your own understanding and application of knowledge in your workplace. For example, an equal opportunities policy says nothing about how you as an assessor use this in your everyday work. It would be much better to show this to your assessor in your workplace, and talk through how it impacts on your work.

See Figure 10.1 for an evidence checklist for V1.

- Portfolio of evidence relating to the internal verifier's relationship with the awarding body, including details of its internal verification strategy relating to a particular award
- Internal verification portfolio for one external verification, relating to signing off of candidate achievement, and showing evidence of the internal verifier making satisfactory support arrangements for assessors, and that the internal verifier's systems documentation and evidence have been acceptable to the external verifier
- Record of observing assessor performance for at least two assessors on two occasions, each with different candidates on all the four occasions; to include the observation of provisional feedback to candidates, and to include written records
- Record of IV being monitored by external verifier *or* qualified second internal verifier, plus written report by monitor
- Sampling framework for at least two assessors, plus external verifier reports indicating that assessor support arrangements are satisfactory

---

Figure 10.1   Evidence checklist for V1

ENSURING THAT YOUR EVIDENCE COVERS THE STANDARDS

The assessment planning process for each unit will have involved you and your primary assessor in discussions about how you will show that you meet all the relevant unit requirements. Your job is to make sure you carry out the agreed assessment activities to the correct standards, and the assessor's job is to check that these activities are satisfactory. In order to do this, the assessor needs to review the evidence you present, whether documentary or process, against the performance criteria/performance indicators, scope/range and knowledge and understanding of each unit to be assessed.

It will be helpful if you state, with each piece of evidence, whether it is an artefact, documentation or 'live' activity, and what criteria, etc you *believe* it covers and why. Your assessor will need to review the evidence and make a record of exactly what you have met, prior to giving you feedback. You should have a copy of this record. If you are able to provide evidence to your assessor regularly, then your coverage of the standards can be built up cumulatively.

QUALITY ASSURANCE OF YOUR EVIDENCE

Internal verification

The assessment centre's internal verifier (IV) may wish to sample your evidence at any point in the assessment process. The IV should *never* be one of your assessors, as this would compromise the integrity of the assessment process. It is possible that the IV may wish to speak to you about the assessment process you are undergoing, or have undergone, and could ask to be present while you are being assessed so that the assessment practice of your own assessor(s) can be monitored. If your portfolio is included in the centre's sampling process, the IV will initial and date the evidence and assessments he or she has checked, using red ink.

External verification

The role of the external verifier (EV) is explained in Chapter 3 and the standards external verifiers practise to are in Chapter 7. External verifiers generally monitor NVQ centres twice a year, so it is likely that an external verification will occur while you are working through your award. The EV may request to see the assessments made by your assessor, together with your evidence, as part of his or her sampling process. EVs use green ink to show their audit trail. Centres normally retain completed candidates' portfolios until after the next external visit.

Certification

After you have been assessed as competent, your assessor will fill in the required documentation necessary for an application for certification to be made. Usually, it is the relevant administrative staff at the centre who will submit the required documentation to the awarding body. You will have provided information such as your date of birth and the name that you wish to have printed on the certificate when you register with the awarding body at the start of your assessment process. Tell the centre if you have previously registered with the same awarding body for another qualification, since some awarding bodies now give candidates a 'unique' number for life. The time taken between a centre applying for certification and the receipt of certificates can take several weeks. Clarify with the centre what happens once it receives the certificate; some centres post them to candidates and others prefer you to call, for security reasons.

A FINAL WORD

For many candidates, getting your assessor or verifier award is a bit like taking your advanced driving test. One might have been driving satisfactorily for years, but it is only during advanced driving training that errors of performance that have crept in over the years are shown up and corrected. The passing of the advanced driving test confirms that the driver is meeting the most rigorous driving standards. Drivers who have passed the test are encouraged to maintain their performance by attending additional training and by retesting every so often. In the same way, and as with many professions, you will need to show regular updating of your competence both as an assessor or verifier, and as a practitioner in your area of vocational competence. Employed staff are likely to have their records of planned and past continuous professional development (CPD) kept by their organizations, but if you are self-employed you will need to keep your own CPD record.

Your certificate qualifies you to practise as an assessor or internal verifier. You are now seen as a 'guardian' of the standards and of the internal quality assurance system of your centre. The reputation of NVQs rests with all of us who are qualified, and perhaps particularly with internal verifiers. Awarding bodies and ENTO provide constant support to those involved with competence-based assessment, via newsletters, Web sites and training, and hopefully you will be able to make time to use their support facilities.

Who knows, in time you may end up as an external verifier, needing to take V2!

SUMMARY

This chapter should have helped you:

- understand the nature of the 'portfolio';
- make best use of the resources available to you;
- consider how to prepare for summative assessment;
- know what happens in internal verification of your evidence;
- understand how external verification and certification will be undertaken.

Appendix 1

Qualification Structures for S/NVQs in Learning and Development

The qualification structure in Learning and Development comprises six S/NVQs at levels 3, 4 and 5. Three of these qualifications have been developed in partnership with government, training companies and employers to raise the standard of delivery of those practitioners and organizations that deliver government-funded training programmes. These are identified with an asterisk (*).

LEVEL 3 IN LEARNING AND DEVELOPMENT

Eleven units

Seven mandatory units:

G3	Evaluate and develop own practice
L3	Identify individual learning aims and programmes
L5	Agree learning programmes with learners
L6	Develop training sessions

L9	Create a climate that promotes learning
L16	Monitor and review progress with learners
L18	Respond to changes in learning and development

Plus two optional units from:

L10	Enable learning through presentations
L11	Enable learning through demonstrations and instructions
L12	Enable individual learning through coaching
L13	Enable group learning

Plus two optional units from:

L4	Design learning programmes
L7	Prepare and develop resources to support learning
L14	Support learners by mentoring in the workplace
L15	Support and advise individual learners
L20	Support competence achieved in the workplace
L23	Support how basic skills are delivered in the workplace
L24	Support people learning basic skills in the workplace
A1	Assess candidates using a range of methods
A2	Assess candidates' performance through observation

LEVEL 3 IN DIRECT TRAINING AND SUPPORT*

Nine units

Six mandatory units:

G3	Evaluate and develop own practice
L3	Identify individual learning aims and programmes
L5	Agree learning programmes with learners

L6	Develop training sessions
L16	Monitor and review progress with learners
L9	Create a climate that promotes learning

Two from option set A:

L10	Enable learning through presentations
L11	Enable learning through demonstrations and instructions
L12	Enable individual learning through coaching
L13	Enable group learning

One from option set B:

L14	Support learners by mentoring in the workplace
L15	Support and advise individual learners
A1	Assess candidates using a range of methods
L20	Support competence achieved in the workplace
H+S D	Review health and safety procedures in the workplace

Alternative: three from option set A and none from option set B.

LEVEL 4 IN LEARNING AND DEVELOPMENT

Twelve units

Eight mandatory units:

G2	Contribute to learning within the organisation
G3	Evaluate and develop own practice
L4	Design learning programmes
L5	Agree learning programmes with learners
L8	Manage the contribution of other people to the learning process

L9	Create a climate that promotes learning
L17	Evaluate and improve learning and development programmes

Either L3 or L2:

L3	Identify individual learning aims and programmes
L2	Identify the learning and development needs of the organisation

Plus four optional units from:

L7	Prepare and develop resources to support learning
L13	Enable group learning
L14	Support learners by mentoring in the workplace
L15	Support and advise individual learners
L16	Monitor and review progress with learners
L18	Respond to changes in learning and development
L19	Provide learning and development in international settings
L21	Plan how to provide basic skills in the workplace
L22	Introduce training for basic skills in the workplace
A1	Assess candidates using a range of methods
A2	Assess candidates' performance through observation
V1	Conduct internal quality assurance of the assessment process

LEVEL 4 IN MANAGEMENT OF LEARNING AND DEVELOPMENT PROVISION*

Eight units, six mandatory:

L1	Develop a strategy and plan for learning and development
P2	Develop a strategy and plan to provide all people resources for the organisation
L2	Identify the learning and development needs of the organisation

L17	Evaluate and improve learning and development programmes
G3	Evaluate and develop own practice
C13 (MSC)	Manage the performance of teams and individuals

Plus two optional units from:

L3	Identify individual learning aims and programmes
L4	Design learning programmes
L8	Manage the contribution of other people to the learning process
L7	Prepare and develop resources to support learning
V1	Conduct internal quality assurance of the assessment process
B3 (MSC)	Manage the use of financial resources
H+S D	Review health and safety procedures in the workplace

LEVEL 4 IN CO-ORDINATION OF LEARNING AND DEVELOPMENT PROVISION*

Seven units

Six mandatory units:

L3	Identify individual learning aims and programmes
L4	Design learning programmes
L5	Agree learning programmes with learners
L8	Manage the contribution of other people to the learning process
L17	Evaluate and improve learning and development programmes
G3	Evaluate and develop own practice

Plus one optional unit from:

L9	Create a climate that promotes learning
L7	Prepare and develop resources to support learning
L15	Support and advise individual learners
L16	Monitor and review progress with learners
L2	Identify the learning and development needs of the organisation
V1	Conduct internal quality assurance of the assessment process
H+S D	Review health and safety procedures in the workplace

LEVEL 5 IN LEARNING AND DEVELOPMENT

Twelve units

Eight mandatory units:

G2	Contribute to learning within the organisation
G3	Evaluate and develop own practice
L1	Develop a strategy and plan for learning and development
L2	Identify the learning and development needs of the organisation
L18	Respond to changes in learning and development
P8	Develop a strategy and plan for the promotion of equality of opportunity and diversity
A7 (MSC)	Establish strategies to guide the work of your organisation

Either B5 or B3:

B5 (MSC)	Secure financial resources for your organisation's plans
B3 (MSC)	Manage the use of financial resources

Plus four optional units from:

L4	Design learning programmes
L8	Manage the contribution of other people to the learning process
C13 (MSC)	Manage the performance of teams and individuals
A8 (MSC)	Evaluate and improve organisational performance
P13	Design, deliver and evaluate changes to organisational structure
C11 (MSC)	Develop management teams
L17	Evaluate and improve learning and development programmes

Appendix 2

The NVQ Code of Practice Tariff of Sanctions

This is found as appendix 4 in the NVQ Code of Practice, and all assessors and verifiers should be thoroughly familiar with it. The tariffs are applied when a centre falls out of compliance with some aspect of the approved centre criteria. There are five levels of tariff, which relate to the element of risk that non-compliance has for candidate certification and centre quality assurance.

On each visit to an NVQ centre, the external verifier will complete an action plan. The action points in the plan will normally relate to the non-compliance with centre approval criteria that will have been approved (and updates where appropriate by formal notification) by the awarding body. If action points produced on one visit have not been addressed by the required date (often, but not necessarily, the date of the next visit), the response of the awarding body will normally be to apply a response at the next level up.

In considering the tariff applications, the external verifier will consider the following points:

- combinations of non-compliance;
- the persistence with which faults fail to be rectified;
- the recurrence of non-compliance;
- malpractice.

Tariffs may be higher, depending on the centre's history.

The results of applying tariffs range from the need to comply with an action plan by a specified date through suspension of regulation and/or certification to withdrawal of approval.

Level 1

Where non-compliance is no threat to the integrity of assessment decisions, the lowest level will be applied; the centre will continue to register candidates and certificate them as they complete, without waiting for the visit of the external verifier (also known as 'direct claims status'). The centre will be expected to address the issues by the agreed date.

Level 2

If there is a possibility that some assessment decisions may be unsound, then the centre will be able to register candidates, but all claims for certification will need to be authorized by the external verifier.

Level 3

If the visit reveals areas of non-compliance that pose either a threat to candidates or a real danger of invalid claims for certification, then the centre will have either its registration or certification (or both) suspended until the matters are resolved.

Level 4

The centre may have approval for specific NVQs withdrawn where it is found that management and quality assurance arrangements for specific NVQs have broken down.

Level 5

Centre approval for all NVQs will be withdrawn if management and quality assurance arrangements for all NVQs run by the centre have irretrievably broken down.

Appendix 3

Learning and Development Assessment Strategy

INTRODUCTION

The standards require evidence of consistent occupational competence as defined by the standards, through relevant work activities. A variety of assessment methods should be used to confirm competence as defined in the standards. Assessment of knowledge should be integrated with the assessment of performance wherever possible and appropriate.

The Employment NTO has an Awarding Body Forum, which will implement and review these Assessment Strategy arrangements in the light of the prevailing requirements of the regulatory authorities.

ASSESSMENT OF PERFORMANCE AND KNOWLEDGE IN THE WORKPLACE

All evidence must be derived from performance within the workplace, with certain exceptions (see Table A3.1). The standards relating to these aspects of competence have been identified and specific forms of assessment attached to them as part of the assessment guidance. Table A3.1 provides a summary of the relevant elements.

Table A3.1

Element and criterion	Preferred form of assessment
L5.1. h)	Assessor questioning using hypothetical context
L5.2. d)	Assessor questioning using hypothetical context
L6.1. c)	Assessor questioning as to alternatives considered
L7.1. e) and f)	Candidate presentation of the ILT alternatives considered
L7.2. h)	Assessor questioning of selection of materials against equality and diversity criteria
L7.2. i)	Assessor questioning on checks conducted to ensure training facilities meet HSEP requirements
L8.3. e)	Assessor questioning using hypothetical context
L9.3. c), d), e), and f)	Assessor questioning using hypothetical context
L12.2 b)	Candidate presentation of the ILT alternatives considered
L13.1. e) and g)	Assessor questioning using hypothetical context
L15.2. d)	Candidate presentation of the ILT alternatives considered
L15.2. h)	Assessor questioning using hypothetical context

SIMULATED WORKING CONDITIONS

Performance of real work activities in the real working environment means that none of the performance criteria in the standards requires the use of simulations.

EXTERNAL QUALITY CONTROL: INDEPENDENT ASSESSMENT

Independent external assessment will require candidates to present a balance of evidence, which must include a substantive component that has been assessed by someone who is independent of the candidate. Substantive is defined here as a primary piece of outcome evidence for one or more units of competence. Independence is defined here as a competent job holder who is qualified as an assessor but will not act as the candidate's primary assessor.

REQUIREMENTS FOR OCCUPATIONAL COMPETENCE OF ASSESSORS AND VERIFIERS

Assessors

All assessors selected by centres must have sufficient occupational competence to ensure an up-to-date working knowledge and experience of the principles and practices specified in the standards they are assessing. 'Sufficient occupational competence' is defined as:

- having held a post for a minimum of one year within the last two years which involved performing the activities defined in the standards as an experienced practitioner;

or:

- being an experienced trainer or instructor of at least one year's standing in the competence area of the standards;

and for both of the above:

- having demonstrated updating within the last year involving at least two of the following activities:
  - work placement;
  - job shadowing;
  - technical skills update training;
  - attending courses;
  - studying for learning and development units;
  - study related to job role;
  - collaborative working with awarding bodies;
  - examining;
  - qualifications development work;
  - other appropriate occupational activity as agreed with the internal verifier.

All assessors will have a sound working knowledge of the content of the standards they are assessing and their assessment requirements. All assessors will either hold the relevant qualification for assessors of national occupational standards or have a development plan indicating progress towards that qualification.

Assessors of assessor-candidates are required to have achieved their relevant assessor unit(s) before they can start to assess assessor-candidates. Similarly, assessors of internal and external verifier candidates need to have achieved their own assessor and verifier units before they can start to assess verifier-candidates.

Internal verifiers

All internal verifiers will have sufficient experience of having conducted assessment of the specific national occupational standards they are verifying or in an appropriate and related occupational area. 'Sufficient occupational competence' is defined as:

- having been an assessor for the standards being assessed, or for a set of standards in a related occupational area, for a minimum of one year within the last two years;

and:

- having demonstrated updating within the last year involving at least two of the following activities:
  - attending awarding body verification training courses;
  - studying for learning and development units;
  - study related to job role;
  - collaborative working with awarding bodies;
  - qualifications development work;
  - other appropriate occupational activity as agreed with the external verifier.

All internal verifiers will have direct responsibility and quality control of assessments of the occupational standards or the quality assurance of the assessment process within an assessment centre that has been approved by an awarding body. All internal verifiers will have a sound working knowledge of assessment and verification principles as defined in the national standards for internal quality assurance and the particular internal verification requirements. All internal verifiers will either hold the relevant qualification for internal verifiers of national occupational standards, or have a development plan indicating progress towards that qualification.

Internal verifiers of assessor-candidates are required to have achieved their internal verification unit before they can start to internally verify assessor-candidates. Similarly, internal verifiers of internal and external verifier candidates need to have achieved their own assessor and verifier units before they can start to internally verify verifier-candidates.

External verifiers

All external verifiers will be drawn from experienced senior practitioners in the broad occupational area of the standards they will verify. 'Experienced senior practitioner' is defined as:

- having held posts of responsibility involving the monitoring and review of the occupational competence of others;

or:

- having been responsible for internal verification and assessment of national occupational standards;

and for both of the above:

- having demonstrated updating and continuing competence within the last year involving at least two of the following activities:

  - attending at least one external verifier induction/training event run by an awarding body;
  - shadowing an experienced external verifier on centre visits;
  - collaborative working with awarding bodies such as redevelopment of external monitoring systems;
  - study related to job role.

All external verifiers will have a sound working knowledge and experience of vocational assessment. They must also be familiar with internal as well as external verification procedures as defined in the national standards for external quality assurance. They must also demonstrate competence in the particular external verification procedures set down by the awarding body for the qualification (including appeals and complaints procedures).

All external verifiers will either hold the relevant qualification for external verifiers of national occupations standards, or have a development plan indicating progress towards that qualification.

External verifiers of assessor-candidates are required to have achieved their external verification unit before they can start to externally verify assessor-candidates. Similarly, external verifiers of internal and external verifier candidates need to have achieved their own assessor and external verifier unit(s) before they can start to externally verify verifier-candidates.

Appendix 4

Frequently asked questions from the Employment National Training Organisation Web site

ENTO is constantly responding to queries from assessors and verifiers via its online service The Learning Network. As a result of this, a regularly updated list of frequently asked questions (FAQs) is accessible to users of the site, and can help minimize unnecessary contact. A selection of FAQs follows:

4. The assessment strategy requires that an assessor must have one year's experience in the past two years in the activities described in the standards. When does this one-year period commence from?

The one year's experience starts from certification of the assessor unit.

7. Does the second assessor or independent assessor need to be independent of the centre?

No, the requirement is for the second assessor to be independent of the candidate and primary assessor but not necessarily independent of the centre, although this may be the case in some instances where an organization uses peripatetic assessors.

11. Who decides on appropriate CPD [continuous professional development] for assessors and verifiers?

The requirement for CPD activity for assessors and internal verifiers must be part of the internal verification strategy and planned in advance. Evidence of the activity must be retained as proof; a certificate of attendance is not evidence of CPD. This would have to be accompanied by some form of evaluation of the activity by the assessor or verifier.

12. Who approves and monitors the planned activity?

The planned CPD activity should be agreed with the external verifier for the awards and monitored by the verifier during normal centre visits. In all cases, all CPD activity should be recorded.

21. Can the assessor of the A&V units be 'working towards'?

No, all assessors and verifiers (internal and external) of the assessment and verification units must themselves hold the appropriate units.

25. Can non-NVQ evidence be used to achieve the assessment and verification units?

In some cases, non-NVQ evidence may be accepted where this evidence is gathered in the workplace. However, you must seek the approval of your awarding body prior to using this type of evidence.

30. Element A1.4 requires the assessor-candidate to contribute to internal quality assurance processes. What does this actually require the assessor-candidate to do?

In the main, this requires the assessor-candidate to comply with internal procedures relating to quality assurance. It also requires the assessor-candidate to contribute to an internal standardization meeting. An internal standardization meeting will normally involve all assessors for a particular qualification and their internal verifier. At the meeting, evidence produced by candidates and judgements made by the assessors will be compared to ensure that there is a level of consistency and that the decisions being made meet national standards across the team. Equally, there will be consideration of evidence that has been deemed not to meet the national standard. The meeting might focus on a particular unit, an assessment method or a type of evidence.

39. Is L20 an assessment unit?

L20 is *not* an assessment unit but is suited to those individuals working with candidates in the workplace who are able to ensure that the candidate has the breadth of experience and opportunity to achieve the units of his or her chosen qualification. In addition, the unit supports the role of witness testimony, but is not required for a witness testimony to be valid.

The view of ENTO is that where possible those supporting candidates in the workplace and as a result providing vital witness testimony should achieve unit L20.

42. What must be included in an internal verifier's sampling strategy for an N/SVQ?

Over a period of time, the following must be sampled by the internal verifier:

- all candidates;
- all units including those that have been assessed by the independent assessor;
- all locations where assessment occurs;
- all assessment methods;
- all assessors responsible to the internal verifier.

Appendix 5

Certificate Awards in Learning and Development

The process of developing S/NVQs in Learning and Development also identified a range of smaller clusters of units that would be valuable to employers and practitioners. These 'clusters' of Learning and Development units are therefore grouped as certificates.

Some of these certificates have been developed as part of the work to raise minimum standards of trainers' delivery of government-funded work-based learning. These certificates, along with the full S/NVQs, are recognized by government as the way forward to raise the quality of training in the workplace. They are indicated below with an asterisk (*).

The certificates below marked with a double asterisk (**) are supported by the Adult Basic Skills Strategy Unit of Department for Education and Skills, with Units L21–L24 having been developed in conjunction with the Basic Skills Agency.

The Employment NTO will support awarding bodies that propose any of these combinations of units as certificates so long as there is a substantial element of assessment that takes place in the workplace.

CERTIFICATE IN INITIAL ASSESSMENT AND SUPPORT OF LEARNERS*

Four units, three mandatory:

G3	Evaluate and develop own practice
L3	Identify individual learning aims and programmes
L5	Agree learning programmes with learners

One from:

L14	Support learners by mentoring in the workplace
L15	Support and advise individual learners
L16	Monitor and review progress with learners

CERTIFICATE IN REVIEW AND ASSESSMENT OF LEARNING*

A1	Assess candidates using a range of methods
G3	Evaluate and develop own practice
L16	Monitor and review progress with learners

CERTIFICATE IN BASIC SKILLS DEVELOPMENT IN THE WORKPLACE*

G3	Evaluate and develop own practice
L21	Plan how to provide basic skills in the workplace
L22	Introduce training for basic skills in the workplace

CERTIFICATE IN BASIC SKILLS SUPPORT IN THE WORKPLACE**

G3	Evaluate and develop own practice
L23	Support how basic skills are delivered in the workplace
L24	Support people learning basic skills in the workplace

CERTIFICATE IN MENTORING IN THE WORKPLACE

G3	Evaluate and develop own practice
L14	Support learners by mentoring in the workplace
L15	Support and advise individual learners
L16	Monitor and review progress with learners

CERTIFICATE IN COACHING LEARNERS IN THE WORKPLACE

G3	Evaluate and develop own practice
L12	Enable individual learning through coaching
L15	Support and advise individual learners
L16	Monitor and review progress with learners

CERTIFICATE IN TRAINING AND PRESENTING IN THE WORKPLACE

G3	Evaluate and develop own practice
L4	Design learning programmes
L6	Develop training sessions
L13	Enable group learning

CERTIFICATE IN SKILLS TRAINING IN THE WORKPLACE

G3	Evaluate and develop own practice
L4	Design learning programmes
L6	Develop training sessions
L11	Enable learning through demonstrations and instructions

CERTIFICATE IN WORKPLACE LEARNING

G3	Evaluate and develop own practice
L9	Create a climate that promotes learning
L11	Enable learning through demonstrations and instructions
L20	Support competence achieved in the workplace

Appendix 6

Employment National Training Organisation Learning and Development Catalogue

A1   Assess candidates using a range of methods
A2   Assess candidates' performance through observation
V1   Conduct internal quality assurance of the assessment process
V2   Conduct external quality assurance of the assessment process
L1   Develop a strategy and plan for learning and development
L2   Identify the learning and development needs of the organisation
L3   Identify individual learning aims and programmes
L4   Design learning programmes
L5   Agree learning programmes with learners
L6   Develop training sessions
L7   Prepare and develop resources to support learning
L8   Manage the contribution of other people to the learning process
L9   Create a climate that promotes learning
L10 Enable learning through presentations
L11 Enable learning through demonstrations and instruction
L12 Enable individual learning through coaching
L13 Enable group learning
L14 Support learners by mentoring in the workplace
L15 Support and advise individual learners
L16 Monitor and review progress with learners

L17 Evaluate and improve learning and development programmes
L18 Respond to changes in learning and development
L19 Provide learning and development in international settings
L20 Support competence achieved in the workplace
L21 Plan how to provide basic skills in the workplace
L22 Introduce training for basic skills in the workplace
L23 Support how basic skills are delivered in the workplace
L24 Support people learning basic skills in the workplace

Glossary

All terms are commonly used in training; there is an emphasis on terms related to assessment.

access (to assessment) Making sure that candidates can be assessed in the most appropriate ways; ensuring that barriers to assessment are minimized; enabling candidates to have some control over the assessment process.

accreditation The formal recognition of a candidate's work against prescribed criteria; candidates can be accredited for all or part of a unit, or in all or part of an award.

accreditation centre *see* **centre**. Also AAC, ADAC.

accreditation of prior learning (APL) The formal recognition of work done previously that is eligible to count towards an award; this work can be from both certificated sources, eg qualifications, and uncertificated sources, eg from previous experience (also: accreditation of prior experimental learning (APEL); accreditation of prior achievement (APA)).

achievement The amount of skill, knowledge or understanding that an individual is able to demonstrate.

action plan The tasks an individual needs to undertake to reach particular goals. Plans usually include target and review dates, may cover any time period, include one or more goals, and may be recorded on formal documentation or be in note form; usually agreed with a supervisor or mentor after review against required standards for an award.

assessment (competence-based) Judging the degree to which a candidate has met predetermined criteria; candidates must show that they can do certain tasks in a prescribed way and that they know the context of the task and why it must be performed in certain ways.

assessment centre *see* **centre**

assessment criteria The standards against which assessments are judged. They must be explicit before the assessment is agreed and undertaken; they determine the minimum of what must be taught, if part of a programme of learning.

assessment instruments Not some medieval torture device, but the range of questionnaires, tests, checklists and other materials used to assess specific skills, knowledge, qualities or understanding. For example, there are tests designed to pick out weaknesses in grammar, or count the number of facts remembered, or tell us how confident we are; languages can be tested through the use of specially designed audiotapes, and skills by using real or simulated work tasks.

assessment opportunities The range of options to candidate and assessor to determine competence or achievement. These may be either work-based or training centre/college-based; they may be formally planned, occur during normal work, and be based on a whole range of sources of evidence. Candidates and assessors need to be aware that there may be alternative opportunities for assessment, other than those normally used.

assessment plan An agreed detailed, written statement between candidate and assessor(s) of how the candidate will demonstrate competence. NVQ assessors should negotiate with their candidates one plan for each unit to be assessed. Plans need to specify as a minimum what will be assessed, the methods to be used, the criteria for assessment, how the assessment will be undertaken and by whom, the timescale and people involved and any special arrangements that need to be made. Assessment plans can be for individuals or for groups.

assessment record A document produced by either an assessor, an organization or an awarding body that records the assessed progress of a candidate against outcomes. It should give sufficient detail that the assessor knows what, how and when the outcomes have been reached.

assessor-devised questions Questions composed by the assessor as opposed to being drawn from a bank of prepared questions produced by, for example, an awarding body.

assignment A practical or written task given to a candidate that tests skills, knowledge or understanding, or combinations of all three. Tasks should be explicit, and candidates should be clear about what is required of them.

authentic Refers to evidence that can be established as relating to the candidate rather than another, or a group. If group work is used as evidence, the candidate's contribution should be clearly identifiable.

award A certificate or record of achievement issued by an awarding body which confirms accreditation. In the case of the 'Assessor and Verifier' awards and mini-awards, the awarding bodies have identified one or more units from the Learning and Development standards and offered them as a 'package'. Some of the awards consist of units that form part of a full NVQ.

awarding body A body (organization) that gives awards, eg Edexcel, the Royal Society of Arts, the Construction Industry Training Board. All awarding bodies that give NVQs (including the assessor and verifier awards) must first be approved by the NCVQ.

barrier (to access) Anything (physical or mental) that prevents a candidate from taking up opportunities for training or assessment.

candidate A person who is preparing to be assessed for an award. In this book the term is used to indicate anyone who is presenting themselves for assessment, eg someone being assessed for NVQs within the workplace, or someone being assessed for GNVQs in a school. Depending on the context, the candidate can be an employee, client, trainee, student or pupil.

candidate- (student-)centred Refers to any approach in training and assessment that considers the needs of the candidate, and that involves the candidate in making choices about the processes to be used.

candidate report A term used in range statements to indicate oral or written reports from the candidate that involve descriptions of activities and processes and some self-assessment, eg a work diary.

centre An organization approved by an awarding body to assess and accredit on its behalf; its advisers, assessors and the awarding body should also approve all internal verifiers.

certification The process of registration, assessment, recording results, completing documentation, applying for and receiving certificates.

competence The ability to perform within a work-related function or occupational area to national standards expected in employment.

contingency An unexpected occurrence that can happen at work, which a candidate will need to show that he or she can deal with. A candidate's competence in dealing with contingencies is often explored through use of questioning, eg 'what if. . .?'questions. Simulations may be another means by which the candidate can be assessed.

continuous assessment Making judgements on a candidate's performance or ability over a period of time.

Core Skills *see* **Key Skills**

credit accumulation An arrangement that enables candidates to collect individual units or elements of competence over a period of time; these can then be matched and accredited against appropriate awards or qualifications. Reassessment does not have to take place should a credit be used for credit transfer; many Credit Accumulation and Transfer Schemes (CATS) already exist in higher education and in future will be used in further education as well.

credit transfer Using credits (units, qualifications) from one award to count towards another different (but usually related) award.

criterion-referenced judgement A judgement made against agreed criteria.

currency Refers to evidence which shows that the candidate can perform competently at the time of the assessment. Currency often depends on the subject: for example, computing changes quickly, bricklaying techniques less swiftly. Evidence less than two years old is usually required, but all cases need to be individually negotiated.

curriculum All the aspects of learning, including methods, resources and syllabus content, that make up a programme of study.

differing sources of evidence *see* **diverse evidence**

direct assessment Assessing a product or process, eg a cake, a completed stock sheet, a training session.

direct evidence Evidence that candidates have produced themselves.

direct support Help that is offered directly to the candidate, eg an offer of advice.

diverse evidence Evidence drawn from a number of different sources, including natural performance; see range for D33.

element (of an award) A description of a set of assessable outcomes. A number of elements make up each NVQ unit; all elements of a unit must have been satisfactorily assessed before a unit award is given, an element being an identifiable or complete task within a unit.

endorsed assessment plan An assessment plan countersigned by a recognized assessor; the endorsement could relate to the original plan, or subsequent modifications after review with a candidate.

evaluation judging A process of determining the value of something as judged through gathering data from a variety of sources (eg interviews, questionnaires, informal discussions, results) and analysing this feedback.

evidence Information from a variety of sources that proves a candidate's competence. The word is occasionally used as a verb, when it refers to the process of logging relevant activities as evidence.

experiential learning Learning that has happened through and from experience, as opposed to formal programmes of education or training. Much adult learning occurs in this way, and the learner often needs help to recognize skills, knowledge and understanding gained in non-formal ways.

external assessment Assessment by an assessor who is not part of (is external to) the assessment or accreditation centre.

external auditing and sampling Auditing and sampling normally carried out to the specifications of an awarding body by an external verifier or moderator. It will follow a process agreed with the external auditor, and will normally involve sampling a range of assessment and internal verification/moderation practice and procedures.

external verifier A person appointed by the awarding body who approves assessment centres and then regularly monitors their operation to national standards. This person acts as a quality assurance link between the approved centre and the awarding body.

fairness Refers to the ensuring of just and equitable conditions in the assessment process for all candidates, eg by providing for candidates with special assessment needs, and by following the national standards for assessment.

feedback reviewing A process of giving constructive oral or written comment to candidates so that they understand the strengths and weaknesses of their performance/evidence and understand what to do as a consequence.

formative assessment Assessment made to help determine future actions and development, or to confirm progress.

functional analysis The process of breaking down a whole job or task into its component pieces according to the different tasks performed in that job. NVQ competences have been determined through the process of functional analysis.

General National Vocational Qualification (GNVQ) A vocationally related qualification covering a broad-based occupational area and aimed primarily at 16- to 19-year-olds in full-time education.

generic competence A competence that occurs across many occupational areas, eg competence in maintaining standards of safety, or competence in working with people. Competence in assessment is a generic competence, as individuals have to be able to assess as part of their job role within every occupational area.

indirect support Help for a candidate that is organized from another source, eg by putting the candidate in touch with someone who could train him or her in certain techniques.

internal assessment Assessment by an assessor who is a member of staff of the assessment or accreditation centre with which the candidate is registered.

internal verifier A person approved by the external verifier to co-ordinate the assessment processes and practices within a centre, and who liaises with the external verifier and the awarding bodies.

Key Skills (previously Core Skills) A set of generic skills transferable across all occupational areas. Key Skills are incorporated into all GNVQ programmes, with mandatory units on communications, application of numbers and information technology, and optional units on personal skills (working with others, and improving own learning and performance) and problem-solving. They can also be used as free-standing units or in conjunction with NVQs.

knowledge evidence A means of showing that candidates know and understand both what they are doing and the context in which they are working. Knowledge evidence is also a means of showing that the candidate knows what to do in a range of different situations.

level (of qualification) NVQs have five levels, from basic competence (level 1) to strategic management (level 5). The levels are determined by job role and are defined on the basis of the skill, knowledge and understanding required, together with the degree of responsibility and supervision involved in performing the related work roles.

log book A document issued by many awarding bodies to candidates in which detailed tasks and tests are set out, together with the required units and elements of competence. Both assessor and candidate are required to sign in the books as competence is confirmed.

moderation A process whereby the results of assessments from more than one source are compared together and against an agreed, accepted standard. Moderation can be internally or externally conducted.

moderator A person approved (by an awarding body, if an external moderator) to conduct moderation, usually with considerable experience in the curriculum area. A moderator often helps with training and with interpretation of the curriculum.

module A self-contained unit of learning that can build towards a qualification. A BTEC leisure studies course might include modules in organizing sporting events and obtaining sponsorship for sport.

National Training Organization (NTO) A body that sets the standards for the industries in its sector, and provides advice and guidance specific to the sector. Soon to be amalgamated into Sector Skills Councils.

National Vocational Qualification (NVQ) A qualification related to employment, recognized by the NVQ, and part of an approved framework of levels. An NVQ *is not* a course in itself; NVQs are awarded when a candidate has successfully demonstrated competence in a required number of units of competence related to job role.

natural performance Refers to the way in which a candidate normally undertakes tasks in the course of his or her employment.

naturally occurring evidence Evidence that occurs as a normal part of an individual's work, ie forms part of their job or part of a programme of study.

norm-referenced assessment Assessment that is judged against the achievements of others undertaking the same assessment. Grades awarded depend on the ability not only of the candidate/student, but also of the whole group under consideration.

occupational standards Set by National Training Organizations, these are standards that have usually been derived by a process of functional analysis. The standards are set for each element of a task within a complete job, and cover the performance, context of operation and underpinning knowledge and understanding required.

open access Refers to systems of learning, training, education or assessment that are open to as many people as possible, as a result of the removal of as many barriers to participation as possible.

open learning Refers to methods of acquiring skills, knowledge and understanding that do not involve traditional attendance at classes and do not even require contact with a tutor. They often involve the use of interactive learning packages (written or video), supplemented by appropriate tutor support.

peer group A group of people equal in status to each other, or from the same or a similar group.

peer report An oral or written description of activities or processes from the candidate's peer group, providing information about the candidate's performance that can be used for assessment purposes.

performance criteria Statements that indicate the standards of performance required for each element of competence. All performance criteria need to be met before an element can be accredited.

performance evidence Evidence from an activity carried out by the candidate, or something produced as a result of that activity.

portfolio A collection of evidence, usually produced over an extended period of time, and from various sources, that is presented together as a demonstration of achievement. The term is sometimes used to indicate the receptacle in which the evidence is contained, eg a ring binder.

pre-set test Any oral or written test prepared in advance by an assessor or by an awarding body. Pre-set tests often form an integral part of assessment for all candidates at particular levels. They are often set out in candidates' log books or are provided separately by the awarding body.

prior experience Experience acquired by the candidate before registering for an assessment that may provide evidence against units or elements.

prior learning Learning acquired by the candidate before registering for an assessment or training programme. This learning may or may not be certificated.

pro forma A template document devised to record a particular stage of a process or procedure.

professional discussion A recorded dialogue held between candidate and assessor. The assessor will plan for the areas that need to be covered, but this is *not* a question-and-answer session, and ideally will be candidate-centred. The discussion should allow the candidate to discuss the understanding behind his or her practice, and, if held in the candidate's workplace, can also enable the candidate to, say, present additional documentary evidence or introduce others involved in the assessment to the assessor where evidence has been judged insufficient to meet the standards.

progress review A meeting between assessor and candidate for the purpose of identifying the candidate's progress against action plans. Actions plans updated following a review will identify areas for development and areas of success.

project An extended piece of practical and/or written work involving planning and research and often presented as a report.

qualification A certificate legally provided which indicates that the holder has reached a necessary standard, eg a driving test certificate, an A level.

quality assurance Refers to methods by which standards are regularly checked and monitored; systems which ensure that procedures are done in certain ways, eg BS 5750 (also known as BSEN ISO 9000).

questioning A range of techniques involving written or oral questions designed to elicit knowledge and understanding from candidates.

range statement A description of the context(s) and circumstances in which performance criteria described in the element should be able to be performed by someone competent in the activity.

record of achievement A composite record of a person's varied achievements and learning experiences over a period of time. It typically contains records of formal and informal learning experiences, credits gained, modules studied, reflections on achievements, agreed learning plans and evaluations.

regulatory bodies Official organizations that are responsible for policy. The QCA and its Welsh, Northern Ireland and Scottish sections are responsible for the way in which qualifications and curriculum for education and skills are developed. Key work is modernizing the examinations system, developing the National Curriculum and building better qualifications for the workforce.

reliability The degree to which an assessment can be administered with the same results to others; the consistent ability of the assessment or the assessor to distinguish accurately between competent and non-competent performance.

review The formal or informal process of reflecting on performance, often conducted between an adviser/assessor and a candidate, usually on a one-to-one basis. Used as a basis for planning future activity.

sampling plan Document showing what or who will be sampled, when and by whom; will relate to the sampling strategy devised by an internal verifier.

sampling strategy The basis on which sampling is taking place. It needs to meet awarding bodies' requirements, and it must show the rationale for sampling so that all candidates, assessors, methods of assessment, evidence, locations and assessment judgements are sampled over time. It could also include details of standardization events devised by an internal verifier.

satellite centre An organization that conducts its own assessments under the supervision of a larger approved centre; staff follow the same practices and procedures as those of the approved centre.

Scottish Vocational Qualification (SVQ) The Scottish equivalent of an NVQ, awarded by SCOTVEC.

simulation A realistic exercise set up specifically to assess knowledge, skills or understanding. It should replicate a real work situation and should be used in circumstances in which it would be difficult or costly to assess within the work context (eg firefighting procedure, or dealing with an emergency first-aid situation). The internal verifier should be able to advise on the acceptable use of simulation in consultation with the external verifier. *NB: NO simulation is allowed in Learning and Development awards; National Training Organisations lay down guidelines for activities that can be simulated.*

skill The ability to carry out a task or perform an activity.

special assessment needs *see* **special assessment requirements**

special assessment requirements NVQs and GNVQs emphasize the importance of access to fair and reliable assessment. According to candidates' circumstances, this may involve special arrangements being made, eg in relation to physical access.

standardization of assessment activities Activities designed to check that assessors would make similar judgements on the same evidence.

systems documentation Documentation produced by the awarding body or centre, to record all aspects of the assessment process, including internal verification and quality assurance.

training needs analysis The identification of individual or organizational training needs through a systematic analysis of current skills against future performance requirements.

transferability The ability to relate learning or performance in one area or context to another. For example, a candidate who can measure in metric in a training environment should be able to do so in the workplace using different materials and equipment.

underpinning knowledge/understanding Knowledge or understanding which ensures that tasks are not performed unthinkingly. Rather, it shows that candidates know why things are done in a particular way, and that they have a general and/or specific knowledge about the task overall.

unit (of competence) A group of elements of competence that together constitute a particular work role, and that form the smallest grouping of competence able to be recognized separately for certification towards an award.

unit credit Units within NVQs and GNVQs can be accredited separately; a unit is the smallest amount of achievement or competence that can be submitted to an awarding body for accreditation.

validity An assessment process has validity if it measures what it is supposed to measure.

verification The process of checking that the correct and agreed procedures and systems have been used.

verifier *see* **external verifier** and **internal verifier**

witness testimony A third-party statement confirming competence against specific units/elements.

work-based assessment An assessment conducted in the candidate's workplace or made on evidence produced from or at the workplace.

work-based learning Learning that occurs at the place of work rather than, for example, through attendance on a formal programme of study based in an institution. Some programmes of study do, however, include work-based teaming as part of the course, eg work experience, or sandwich courses.

work-based training Training that takes place within the work environment as opposed to being conducted elsewhere.

Supporting Materials

FURTHER READING

Ainley, P and Corney, M (1990) *Training for the Future: The rise and fall of the MSC*, Cassell, London

Armitage, A *et al* (2003) *Teaching and Training in Post-compulsory Education*, Open University Press, Buckingham

Boam, R and Sparrow, P (1992) *Designing and Achieving Competency*, McGraw-Hill, Maidenhead

Business and Technology Education Council (BTEC) (1990) *The Accreditation of Prior Learning (APL): General guidance*, BTEC, London

BTEC (1993) *Implementing BTEC GNVQs: A guide for centres*, BTEC, London

City & Guilds (1990) *APL Handbook: Guidance on the accreditation of prior learning*, City and Guilds, London

Confederation of British Industry (CBI) (1989) *Towards a Skills Revolution: Report of the vocational education and training taskforce*, CBI, London

Cotton, J (1995) *The Theory of Assessment*, Kogan Page, London

Department for Education and Employment (DfEE) (1996) *Review of 14–19 Curriculum*; final report (chaired by Sir Ronald Dearing), DfEE, Sheffield

DfEE (1996) *Skills, Qualifications and Utilisation: A research review*, DfEE, Sheffield

DfEE (1998) *The Learning Age*, DfEE, London

Department for Education and Skills (DfES) (2002) *Success for All*, Strategy Paper, DfES, London

Ecclestone, K (1996) *How to Assess the Vocational Curriculum*, Kogan Page, London

Edexcel (2003) *Continuous Professional Development*, a conversion pack for assessors and verifiers, Edexcel, London

Etherton, T and Houston, T (1990) *Equal Opportunities: The role of awarding bodies*, NCVQ, London

Evans, B (1992) *The Politics of the Training Market*, Routledge, London

Further Education Unit (FEU) (1992) *TDLB Standards in Further Education*, FEU, London

FEU (1993) *Standards in Action*, FEU, London

Fletcher, S (1992) *NVQs Standards and Competence*, Kogan Page, London

Handy, C (1990) *The Age of Unreason*, Arrow, London

Her Majesty's Stationery Office (HMSO) (1975) *Sex Discrimination Act*, HMSO, London

HMSO (1976) *Race Relations Act*, HMSO, London

HMSO (1986) *Working Together, Education and Training*, Government White Paper, HMSO, London

HMSO (1991) *Education and Training for the Twenty-first Century*, Government White Paper, HMSO, London

HMSO (1994) *Competitiveness: Helping business to win*, Government White Paper, HMSO, London

Hyland, T (1992) Meta-competence, metaphysics and vocational expertise, *Competence and Assessment*, **20**, pp 22–24

Hyland, T. (1999) *Vocational Studies, Lifelong Learning and Social Values: Investigating education, training and NVQs under the New Deal*, Monitoring Change in Education Series, Ashgate, Aldershot

Jessup, G (1990) *Accreditation of Prior Learning in the Context of National Vocational Qualifications*, National Council for Vocational Qualifications, London

Jessup, G (1991) *NVQs and the Emergency Model of Education and Training*, Falmer Press, London

Manpower Services Commission (MSC) (1981) *A New Training Initiative: A consultative document*, MSC, Sheffield

MSC (1981) *A New Training Initiative: An agenda for action*, MSC, Sheffield

MSC and National Economic Development Council (1986) *Review of Vocational Qualifications in England and Wales*, HMSO, London

Mullin, R (1992) *Decisions and Judgements in NVQ-based Assessment*, NCVQ, London

National Council for Vocational Qualifications (NCVQ) (1993) *Awarding Bodies Common Accord*, NCVQ, London.

NCVQ (1994) *Implementing the National Standards for Assessment and Verification*, NCVQ, London

NCVQ (1994) *Non-discriminatory Assessment Practice*, NCVQ, London

NCVQ (1995) *GNVQ Assessment Review*, final report of the review group (chaired by Dr John Capey), NCVQ, London

NCVQ (1995) *NVQ Criteria and Guidance*, NCVQ, London

NCVQ (1996) *Implementing Standards for Assessment and Verification*, 2nd edn, NCVQ, London

NCVQ and SCOTVEC (1996) *Review of Top 100 NVQs* (chaired by Gordon Beaumont), NCVQ, London

NCVQ, Business and Technology Education Council, City & Guilds and Royal Society of Arts (1995) *GNVQ Quality Framework*, NCVQ, London

Ollin, R and Smith, E (1996) *Planning, Delivering and Assessing GNVQs: The complete guide to the GPA units*, Kogan Page, London

Papathomas, A (1990) *Open Access to Assessment for NVQs: New roles for the FE college*, NCVQ, London

Qualifications and Curriculum Authority (QCA) (1999) *Developing and Assessment Strategy for NVQs and SVQs*, QCA Publications, London

Read, Hilary (2004) *Excellence in assessment and verification*, Read-on Publications, ENTO

Rees, I and Walker, S (2000) *Teaching, Training and Learning*, Business Education Publishers, Sutherland

Rowntree, D (1987) *Assessing Students: How shall we know them?*, Kogan Page, London

Simosko, S (1992) *APL: A practical guide for professionals*, Kogan Page, London

Smithers, A (1993) *All Our Futures*, report commissioned for Channel 4 documentary

Stationery Office, The (1999) *Learning to Succeed*, Government White Paper, The Stationery Office, London

Stationery Office (2003) *21st Century Skills: Realising our potential – individuals, employers, nation*, Government White Paper, The Stationery Office, London

Training and Development Lead Body (1992, revised 1994) *National Standards for Training and Development*, HMSO, London

Wolf, A (1993) *Assessment Issues and Problems in a Criterion-based System*, Further Education Unit, London

Wolf, A (1995) *Competence-based Assessment*, Open University Press, Buckingham

USEFUL WEB SITES

Adult Learning Inspectorate: www.ali.gov.uk/htm/index.htm
Assessment and Qualifications Alliance: www.aqa.org.uk/
Association of External Verifiers: www.ava.org.uk/
City & Guilds: www.city-and-guilds.co.uk
Department for Education and Skills: www.dfes.gov.uk
Department for Education and Skills Lifelong Learning: www.lifelonglearning.co.uk/
Department for Work and Pensions: www.dwp.gov.uk/
ENTO: www.ento.co.uk

Edexcel: www.edexcel.org.uk/qualifications/

Federation of Awarding Bodies: www.awarding.org.uk/

Learning and Skills Council: www.lsc.gov.uk/

Learning and Skills Development Agency: www.lsda.org.uk/

Local authority site with publications from six government departments: www.info4local.gov.uk/

Modern Apprenticeships: https://www.realworkrealpay.info/lsc/

New Deal: www.newdeal.co.uk/

NVQ Web site: www.dfes.gov.uk/nvq/

Qualifications and Curriculum Authority (QCA): www.qca.org.uk/

Sector Skills Development Agency: www.ssda.org.uk/

Teachernet: www.teachernet.gov.uk/

Index